Ultimate Beginners Guide to Real Estate Investing Financing

Real Estate Investing, Volume 10

Jim Pellerin

Published by Jim Pellerin, 2023.

ULTIMATE BEGINNERS GUIDE TO REAL ESTATE INVESTING FINANCING

First edition. May 18, 2023.

ISBN: 979-8223790020

Written by Jim Pellerin.

Also by Jim Pellerin

Real Estate Investing

Real Estate Investing Strategies: The Secret to Financial Independence with Real Estate

Real Estate Investing with Lease Options - Investing in Real Estate with No Money Down

Invest Now - The Passive Approach to Winning at Real Estate

The Ultimate Beginners Guide to Real Estate Investing

The 98 Best Real Estate Investing Strategies

The Ultimate Beginners Guide to Wholesale Real Estate Investing

The Ultimate Beginners Guide to Rental Real Estate Investing

The Ultimate Beginners Guide to Fix and Flip Real Estate Investing

The Ultimate Beginners Guide to Private Equity Real Estate Investing

Ultimate Beginners Guide to Real Estate Investing Financing

Watch for more at www.jimpellerin.com.

Table of Contents

.... 1

Why You Should Read This Book.. 3

Chapter 1: Introduction to Real Estate Financing 9

Chapter 2: Types of Real Estate Financing.................................. 23

Chapter 3: Choosing the Right Financing Option 37

Chapter 4: Preparing for Real Estate Financing............................ 49

Chapter 5: Real Estate Financing Process..................................... 61

Chapter 6: Working with a Mortgage Broker................................ 75

Chapter 7: Government-Backed Loans 85

Chapter 8: Using Retirement Accounts for Real Estate Investing 95

Chapter 9: Hard Money and Private Money Loans 105

Chapter 10: Real Estate Investment Partnerships.......................... 121

Chapter 11: Real Estate Financing for Flipping Houses 139

Chapter 12: Financing Multifamily Properties 149

Chapter 13: Financing for Commercial Real Estate 165

Chapter 14: Creative Real Estate Financing Strategies.................. 179

Chapter 15: Real Estate Financing Risks and Challenges................ 199

Chapter 16: Refinancing Your Mortgage 215

Chapter 17: Summary: Real Estate Financing and Investment Goals.. 223

Conclusion: Last Part 237

About The Author 239

Other Books By Jim Pellerin 241

The Ultimate Beginners Guide to Real Estate Investing Financing

An Overiew of Real Estate

Investing Financing

Jim Pellerin

Updated for 2023

Why You Should Read This Book

Most people who want to get started with Real Estate Investing, have no idea how to get sarted. Or worse, they have some idea how to get started but it is the wrong strategy for them.

This book provides an overview of how to get financing for your Real Estate Investments. This book is NOT a practical approach to Real Estate Investing financing and the reader is NOT expected to be able to get real estate financing after completing this book.

In this book, you will learn enough information to be able to get *started* financing your real estate investment.

Learning Method

This book is meant to teach you the information using special information presentation techniques. These techniques will enhance your learning and retention experience.

Most chapters are structured as follows:

1. Tell you what you are going to learn
2. Provide the learning information
3. Tell you what you just leanred

The Ultimate Beginners Guide to Real Estate Investing Financing

Chapter 1: Introduction to Real Estate Financing

Real Estate Financing - Photo by nattanan23

1.1 Understanding Real Estate Financing

Real estate financing is a crucial aspect of the real estate industry, enabling individuals and businesses to acquire, develop, or refinance properties. It encompasses a wide range of methods and sources of funding, each serving a specific purpose and catering to diverse needs. This section aims to provide an in-depth understanding of real estate financing, exploring its types, mechanisms, and significance.

One of the primary forms of real estate financing is a **mortgage**. A mortgage is a loan obtained from a financial institution, typically a bank, specifically for purchasing a property. The property being purchased serves as *collateral* for the loan, providing security for the lender. Mortgages come in various forms, including *fixed-rate mortgages*, *adjustable-rate mortgages,* and *government-backed loans like FHA or VA loans.* The terms of the mortgage, such as the interest rate, repayment period, and down payment requirements, vary based on factors such as the borrower's creditworthiness and the prevailing market conditions.

Another significant aspect of real estate financing is **equity investments**. Equity financing involves raising funds by selling a share of ownership in a property to investors. This type of financing is commonly used in real estate development projects or commercial ventures where substantial capital is required. Investors who contribute equity financing become *partial owners* of the property and are entitled to a share of the profits or rental income generated by the investment. Equity investments can be structured in various ways, such as limited partnerships or real estate investment trusts (REITs), allowing individuals to invest in real estate without directly owning or managing the properties.

Understanding real estate financing is crucial for both buyers and sellers in the real estate market.

1. For **buyers**, having a comprehensive knowledge of financing options enables them to make informed decisions and select the most suitable funding method for their needs. It helps them evaluate the affordability of a property, understand the long-term financial obligations, and assess the risks associated with borrowing.
2. On the other hand, **sellers** benefit from understanding financing options as it expands their pool of potential buyers. By being aware of different financing methods, sellers can attract a wider range of buyers who may have varied financial circumstances and preferences.

Overall, real estate financing plays a pivotal role in facilitating property transactions and driving the growth of the real estate market. It empowers individuals and businesses to invest in properties, develop projects, and generate wealth through real estate ownership. By understanding the various methods and sources of real estate financing, individuals can navigate the complex landscape of property transactions with confidence and make informed decisions that align with their financial objectives.

1.2 Importance of Real Estate Financing

Real estate financing plays a vital role in the real estate industry, serving as a catalyst for property purchases, development projects, and wealth creation. It holds immense importance for individual buyers and investors, enabling them to fulfill their real estate goals and leverage the potential of properties as valuable assets. This section emphasizes the significance of real estate financing and its impact on various stakeholders in the industry.

For individual buyers, real estate financing is often the key to achieving the dream of **homeownership**. Purchasing a property is a substantial financial commitment, and many individuals rely on financing options such as mortgages to make this significant investment. By providing access to funds that can be repaid over an extended period, real estate financing makes homeownership more attainable and manageable for buyers. It allows them to spread the cost of a property over time, rather than needing to pay the full purchase price upfront. Additionally, real estate financing empowers buyers to choose properties that *align with their needs* and preferences, as they can evaluate affordability and negotiate better terms with the assistance of financing.

Real estate financing also plays a crucial role in property **development projects**. Developers often rely on financing options to acquire land, fund construction or renovation activities, and cover operational costs. Without access to financing, many development projects would not come to fruition, stalling the growth and expansion of the real estate market. Financing options such as *construction loans* provide developers with the necessary capital to start and complete projects, stimulating economic activity and creating employment opportunities. Moreover, real estate financing allows developers to leverage their investments, maximizing the potential returns on their projects.

Investors in the real estate market also heavily rely on financing to capitalize on opportunities and generate income streams. By using real estate financing, investors can leverage their capital and **acquire properties** that have the potential to appreciate in value or generate rental income. Financing options like *commercial real estate loans* enable investors to purchase commercial properties, such as office buildings, retail centers, or apartment complexes, which can yield substantial returns over time. Investors can also utilize equity financing methods to pool resources with other investors and participate in larger-scale real estate ventures. This diversifies their portfolio and allows for greater exposure to the real estate market.

Real estate financing **contributes to wealth creation** and long-term **financial security** for both individual buyers and investors. Property ownership has historically been a reliable means of building equity and accumulating wealth. Through real estate financing, individuals can leverage their investment and benefit from potential property appreciation, which can significantly enhance their net worth over time. Investors, too, can generate income through rental properties or capital gains from property sales, providing a steady stream of revenue and long-term financial stability.

In summary, real estate financing holds immense importance in the real estate industry, serving as a vital component for property purchases, development projects, and wealth creation. It empowers individuals to achieve homeownership, facilitates property development, and provides investors with opportunities to generate income and build wealth. By understanding and leveraging real estate financing options, buyers and investors can navigate the market with confidence, unlock the potential of properties, and achieve their financial goals in the dynamic and rewarding world of real estate.

1.3 Types of Real Estate Financing

Real estate financing encompasses a wide range of options, each tailored to specific needs and circumstances. This section provides an overview of some of the different types of real estate financing, including both traditional and non-traditional methods. By understanding the characteristics and considerations associated with each type, individuals can make informed decisions regarding their real estate investments.

Traditional Mortgages

Traditional mortgages are the most common and traditional form of real estate financing. They involve obtaining a loan from a financial institution, typically a bank, where the property being purchased serves as collateral. Mortgages come in various forms, such as *fixed-rate mortgages* and *adjustable-rate mortgages*. Fixed-rate mortgages have a set interest rate and monthly payment throughout the loan term, providing stability and predictability. Adjustable-rate mortgages, on the other hand, have interest rates that may fluctuate over time based on market conditions. Mortgages offer *longer repayment terms*, typically ranging from 15 to 30 years, allowing borrowers to spread out the payments. However, mortgages often require a down payment, and borrowers need to meet certain creditworthiness criteria to qualify.

Commercial Real Estate Mortgages

Commercial real estate loans are specifically designed for businesses and investors seeking financing for commercial properties. These properties can include office buildings, retail centers, industrial complexes, or multifamily housing. Commercial loans often have stricter eligibility requirements compared to residential mortgages. Lenders evaluate:

1. the *financial health of the business or investor*,
2. the property's *potential income-generating capacity*, and
3. the overall market conditions.

Commercial loans may have *higher interest rates* and *shorter repayment terms* than residential mortgages. They may also require a higher down payment and may be subject to additional fees and documentation, including business plans, financial statements, and rent rolls.

Construction Loans

Construction loans provide financing for the construction or renovation of properties. These loans are typically *short-term* and have *higher interest rates* compared to long-term financing options. Construction loans disburse funds in stages, known as draws, based on the progress of the construction project. As construction progresses, borrowers receive funds to cover costs. Once the construction is complete, borrowers can refinance the construction loan into a long-term mortgage or sell the property. Construction loans carry inherent risks, as the value and success of the property depend on the completion of the project within budget and on schedule.

Equity Financing

Equity financing involves raising funds by *selling a share of ownership* in a property to investors. This type of financing is commonly used in real estate development projects or commercial ventures. Equity investors become partial owners of the property and share in the profits or rental income generated by the investment. Equity financing can take various forms, such as *partnerships, joint ventures*, or *real estate investment trusts (REITs)*. It offers the potential for higher returns but also carries risks, including the loss of control over the property's management decisions and the need to distribute profits among investors.

Private Lending and Hard Money Loans

Private lending and hard money loans are alternative financing options provided by private individuals or organizations. These loans are often sought when *traditional financing is not readily available* due to factors like poor credit history or unconventional property types. Private lenders focus more on the value of the property rather than the borrower's creditworthiness. Hard money loans, in particular, are *short-term loans* with *higher interest rates* and more stringent terms. They are typically used for real estate investments that have a quick turnaround, such as fix-and-flip projects.

Each type of real estate financing has its own set of advantages and considerations. Traditional financing options like mortgages offer stability and longer repayment terms, making them suitable for long-term homeownership. Commercial real estate loans cater to businesses and investors with specific property requirements. Construction loans address the financing needs of property development projects. Equity financing allows for shared ownership and potential higher returns. Private lending and hard money are for quick turnaround projects.

1.4 Benefits of Real Estate Investing

Real estate investing offers numerous benefits for individuals and investors looking to enter or expand their presence in the real estate market. This section highlights the advantages of real estate financing and emphasizes the importance of understanding the associated risks.

Leverage

By utilizing financing options such as mortgages or commercial loans, individuals can acquire properties with a smaller upfront investment. This leverage allows investors to control a more *substantial asset* than their initial capital would permit. For example, a buyer who puts down a 20% down payment on a property and finances the remaining 80% through a mortgage effectively controls the entire property's value. If the property appreciates over time, the investor's return on investment is based on the property's total value, not just the initial down payment. Leverage amplifies potential returns and can significantly enhance long-term wealth-building opportunities.

Diversification

Investing solely in traditional financial assets like stocks and bonds can expose investors to market volatility and limited diversification. Real estate, on the other hand, is considered a tangible asset with its own unique characteristics and returns. By allocating a portion of their portfolio to real estate investments, investors can *spread risk across different asset classes* and potentially increase overall portfolio stability. Real estate investments tend to have a low correlation with traditional financial markets, allowing for further diversification and potential *risk reduction*.

Income Generation

Real estate investments have the potential to generate *consistent income streams*. Rental properties, for example, can provide a steady cash flow in the form of monthly rental payments. This income can help cover mortgage payments, property expenses, and generate additional profit. Commercial properties, such as office buildings or retail centers, often offer higher rental yields than residential properties. Real estate financing allows investors to acquire income-generating properties, providing a *reliable source of passive income* and potentially contributing to *long-term financial security.*

Tax Benefits

Real estate provides several tax advantages:

1. *Interest payments* on mortgages and other real estate loans are often tax-deductible.
2. Additionally, investors can take advantage of *depreciation deductions* on rental properties, offsetting taxable rental income.
3. *1031 exchanges*, also known as like-kind exchanges, allow investors to defer capital gains taxes by reinvesting the proceeds from the sale of one property into another similar property.

These tax benefits can have a significant positive impact on an investor's overall return on investment and should be carefully considered and utilized in accordance with local tax regulations.

Wealth Building

As properties appreciate in value over time, investors benefit from *capital appreciation*, increasing their net worth. Through consistent cash flow from rental income and potential tax advantages, real estate investments can generate *substantial returns* and contribute to wealth accumulation. Real estate also offers the potential for active wealth creation through property development projects or value-add strategies, where investors can improve properties and increase their market value.

In summary, real estate investing provides numerous benefits for individuals and investors. Leveraging investments, diversifying portfolios, generating income, and accessing tax advantages contribute to long-term wealth-building opportunities.

1.5 How to Get Started with Real Estate Investing

Getting started with real estate investing requires careful planning, research, and strategic decision-making. This section provides practical guidance on the key steps to take when entering the world of real estate financing.

1. Research the Market:

Before diving into real estate investing, it's crucial to conduct thorough market research. Familiarize yourself with the local real estate market trends, property values, rental demand, and potential growth areas. Understanding the market dynamics will help you identify suitable investment opportunities and make informed financing decisions.

2. Develop a Financing Plan

A financing plan is essential to outline your goals, budget, and the financing options that align with your needs. Determine your *investment objectives*, such as whether you aim to acquire a residential property for personal use or generate rental income from commercial properties. Assess your financial capacity, including your creditworthiness, income, and available funds for down payments and closing costs. With a clear financing plan, you can focus on finding the most suitable financing options for your real estate venture.

3. Find the Right Lender or Investor

Depending on your financing plan and investment goals, identify potential lenders or investors who specialize in the type of financing you require. Banks, credit unions, and mortgage brokers are common sources of traditional mortgage financing. Commercial real estate lenders specialize in funding commercial properties, while private lenders or hard money lenders cater to borrowers with unique circumstances or unconventional properties. If considering equity financing, research real estate investment groups, private equity firms, or crowdfunding platforms. Seek recommendations, read reviews, and compare terms and rates to find a reputable and reliable financing partner.

4. Prepare Documentation

When approaching lenders or investors, be prepared to provide the necessary documentation to support your financing application. This typically includes personal financial statements, tax returns, bank statements, proof of income, and details of the property you intend to finance. For commercial loans, additional documentation, such as business plans, financial projections, and rent rolls, may be required. Organizing and preparing these documents in advance will expedite the financing process and demonstrate your credibility as a borrower or investor.

5. Negotiate Favorable Terms

Once you have identified potential lenders or investors, negotiate the terms and conditions of the financing. Compare interest rates, loan terms, repayment schedules, and any associated fees or charges. For equity financing, carefully consider the ownership structure, profit-sharing arrangements, and exit strategies. Negotiating favorable terms can significantly impact the overall cost and success of your real estate investment. Be prepared to ask questions, seek clarifications, and leverage competing offers to secure the most advantageous financing terms.

6. Seek Professional Advice

Real estate financing can be complex, and seeking professional advice is highly recommended. Consult with a *real estate attorney*, *financial advisor*, or *mortgage broker* to ensure you fully understand the legal and financial implications of your financing decisions. They can help you navigate the intricacies of real estate contracts, review financing agreements, and provide guidance on the best financing options based on your specific circumstances.

7. Perform Due Diligence

Before finalizing any real estate financing agreement, conduct thorough due diligence on the property, the lender or investor, and the terms of the financing. Obtain property *inspections*, *appraisals*, and *title searches* to assess the property's condition, value, and ownership rights. Evaluate the lender's or *investor's track record*, *reputation*, and *financial stability*. Review the financing agreement in detail, including interest rates, repayment terms, prepayment penalties, and any contingencies. Doing your due diligence minimizes potential risks and ensures you are making an informed decision.

Getting started with real estate investing requires careful planning, research, and thorough evaluation of options. By following these steps, conducting due diligence, and seeking professional advice, you can navigate the real estate financing process with confidence and set yourself up for

Conclusion

In conclusion, real estate financing is a fundamental aspect of the real estate industry, offering individuals and investors the means to participate in property ownership, development, and investment. By exploring the different types of financing available, understanding the benefits they offer, and seeking professional advice, you can navigate the complex world of real estate financing with confidence and maximize the opportunities available to you.

Chapter 2: Types of Real Estate Financing

Mortgage - Photo by Towfiqu barbhuiya

2.1 Mortgage Loans: An In-Depth Explanation of Real Estate Financing

The world of real estate financing can be complex, with numerous options available to prospective buyers. Among these options, mortgage loans stand out as one of the most common and widely used methods for financing real estate purchases. This section aims to provide an in-depth explanation of mortgage loans, covering essential aspects such as the loan application process, down payments, interest rates, and various mortgage options available, including fixed-rate and adjustable-rate mortgages.

When it comes to purchasing a home, most buyers require financial assistance in the form of a mortgage loan.

Application Process

The first step in obtaining a mortgage loan is the application process, which involves submitting detailed information about one's *financial status*, including income, assets, and credit history, to a lender. The lender then assesses this information to determine the borrower's creditworthiness and the amount of loan they qualify for. It is crucial for borrowers to be thorough and accurate in their application, as any discrepancies or omissions can result in delays or even loan rejection.

Down Payment

One crucial factor to consider when applying for a mortgage loan is the down payment. This is the *initial payment* made by the borrower towards the purchase of the property. Down payment requirements vary depending on factors such as the lender, the type of loan, and the borrower's financial situation. Generally, a *down payment of 20%* of the property's purchase price is considered ideal, as it allows borrowers to *avoid private mortgage insurance (PMI)* and secure more favorable loan terms. However, it's worth noting that some lenders offer programs with lower down payment requirements, making homeownership more accessible to a broader range of buyers.

Interest rates

play a significant role in mortgage loans, as they determine the cost of borrowing and the total amount the borrower will repay over the life of the loan. There are two primary types of interest rates associated with mortgages, *fixed-rate* and *adjustable-rate*:

1. A **fixed-rate mortgage** offers a consistent interest rate over the entire loan term, providing stability and predictability in

monthly payments.

2. On the other hand, an **adjustable-rate mortgage (ARM)** features an interest rate that can fluctuate over time, typically tied to a specific financial index. ARMs often have lower initial rates, but they can adjust periodically, leading to potential changes in monthly payments.

Government Backed Loans

When considering mortgage options, borrowers can choose from various loan types that suit their financial goals and circumstances. In addition to the *fixed-rate* and *adjustable-rate* mortgages mentioned earlier, other options include government-backed loans like *Federal Housing Administration (FHA) loans* and *Veterans Affairs (VA) loans*, which have specific eligibility criteria and benefits.

1. **FHA loans**, for instance, are designed to assist first-time homebuyers and those with lower credit scores by offering more lenient requirements.
2. **VA loans**, on the other hand, are available to military veterans and active-duty service members, providing competitive interest rates and flexible down payment options.

Mortgage loans are an integral part of real estate financing, enabling individuals and families to achieve the dream of homeownership. This section provided an in-depth explanation of mortgage loans, covering crucial aspects such as the application process, down payments, interest rates, and various mortgage options available. It is essential for prospective borrowers to thoroughly research and understand these factors to make informed decisions about their mortgage financing, ensuring a smooth and successful buying experience.

2.2 Hard Money Loans: Exploring Short-Term Financing

for Real Estate Investments

In the realm of real estate financing, hard money loans have gained popularity as a viable option for investors seeking short-term funding. This section aims to delve into the characteristics of hard money loans, including higher interest rates and shorter repayment periods, and shed light on the situations in which they may be beneficial for borrowers.

Hard money loans, also known as *private money loans*, are typically offered by private investors or lending companies and are primarily used for real estate investments. Unlike traditional mortgage loans, hard money loans are based on the **value of the property** being used as *collateral* rather than the borrower's creditworthiness. This aspect makes hard money loans particularly attractive for individuals with less-than-perfect credit or those who require immediate funding and cannot wait for the lengthy approval process associated with conventional loans.

One notable characteristic of hard money loans is the **higher interest rates** compared to traditional loans. These interest rates can range from *10% to 15% or even higher*, reflecting the increased risk undertaken by the lender. The rationale behind this higher cost is that hard money loans are typically *short-term* in nature, usually lasting from a few months to a couple of years. The lender aims to generate a higher return on their investment during this relatively brief period.

Another important aspect to consider when contemplating hard money loans is the **shorter repayment period**. Unlike traditional mortgage loans that can span 15 to 30 years, hard money loans usually have a repayment term ranging from six months to three years. This shorter timeframe aligns with the intended use of hard money loans, which is *primarily for real estate investors* looking to acquire, renovate, or flip properties for a quick profit. The accelerated repayment period ensures that the lender recoups their investment promptly.

Despite the higher interest rates and shorter repayment periods, hard money loans can be beneficial in certain situations. For instance, real estate investors who need **immediate access to funds** to secure a property or take advantage of time-sensitive investment opportunities can benefit from the speed at which hard money loans can be approved and funded. Additionally, individuals with **less-than-perfect credit** may find it easier to qualify for a hard money loan based on the value of the property they intend to purchase or use as collateral.

Moreover, hard money loans can be advantageous when traditional financing options are not readily available. This could be due to factors such as stringent credit requirements, complex property situations, or the need for quick funding that conventional lenders cannot provide. In such cases, hard money loans can bridge the financing gap and enable borrowers to proceed with their real estate investments.

2.3 Commercial Loans: Financing Solutions for Commercial Properties

When it comes to financing commercial properties such as office buildings, retail spaces, or industrial properties, commercial loans are specifically designed to meet the unique needs of these ventures. This section aims to explore the distinct features of commercial loans, including loan-to-value ratios, underwriting criteria, and repayment structures.

Commercial loans differ from residential mortgage loans in several key aspects. One notable difference is the **property valuation method**. In residential mortgages, lenders often use the *appraised value* of the property to determine the loan amount.

However, in commercial loans, the focus shifts to the property's **income-generating potential**. Lenders typically assess the property's *net operating income (NOI)* to determine the loan amount, with *LTV* *ratios ranging from 65% to 80%* of the property's value. This approach ensures that the property's income can sufficiently cover the loan payments.

Another significant aspect of commercial loans is the **underwriting criteria**. Lenders carefully analyze the *financial viability of the commercial property* and the borrower's *creditworthiness*. In addition to the borrower's *personal financials*, lenders also scrutinize the property's *financial statements*, including rental income, expenses, and occupancy rates. The property's *location, market conditions*, and potential for *future growth* also play a role in the underwriting process. This comprehensive evaluation enables lenders to assess the risk associated with the loan and offer suitable loan terms and interest rates.

Repayment structures for commercial loans are typically different from residential mortgages as well. While residential mortgages often feature long-term amortization periods of 15 to 30 years, commercial loans usually have *shorter terms*, typically ranging from five to 20 years. Additionally, commercial loans may require a *balloon payment*, where a significant portion of the principal is due at the end of the term. This structure allows borrowers to benefit from lower monthly payments during the loan term while ensuring the lender recoups the full loan amount by the end of the loan period.

In summary, commercial loans serve as vital financing solutions for commercial properties, offering specific features tailored to the unique needs of these ventures. From evaluating loan-to-value ratios based on the income-generating potential to comprehensive underwriting criteria and repayment structures, commercial loans provide flexibility and options for borrowers.

2.4 Bridge Loans: Temporary Financing Solutions for Property Transitions

In the world of real estate, bridge loans have emerged as a valuable tool for individuals and investors navigating the transition from one property to another. This section will introduce bridge loans, temporary loans designed to bridge a financing gap during property transitions. It will highlight how bridge loans can be helpful when individuals or investors require immediate funding while awaiting the sale of a property or securing long-term financing.

Bridge loans serve as a **temporary financing solution** that "bridges" the gap between the purchase of a new property and the sale of an existing property. These loans are particularly useful when individuals or investors face *timing challenges*, such as needing funds to secure a new property while still in the process of selling their current property.

Bridge loans provide the necessary *liquidity* during this transitional period, ensuring that borrowers can seize opportunities without being constrained by the sale timeline.

One of the primary benefits of bridge loans is the **ability to access immediate funding**. Traditional financing options, such as mortgage loans, often involve a lengthy approval process, which may hinder individuals or investors from capitalizing on time-sensitive opportunities. Bridge loans, on the other hand, offer a *quicker and more streamlined application process*, allowing borrowers to obtain funds faster. This swift access to financing can be critical in competitive real estate markets or situations where a quick closing is required.

Bridge loans are typically **secured by the collateral of the borrower's existing property**. Lenders evaluate the value of the property and the borrower's ability to repay the loan, taking into account factors such as *creditworthiness*, *income*, and the potential proceeds from the sale of the current property. The loan amount is usually a percentage of the property's appraised value, commonly ranging from 70% to 80%. The repayment of the bridge loan is typically structured as a *balloon payment*, where the full principal and accrued interest are due at the end of the loan term, which usually ranges from six months to three years.

While bridge loans offer immediate funding, it's important to note that they often come with **higher interest rates** compared to traditional mortgage loans. The higher rates reflect the short-term nature of bridge loans and the perceived increased risk taken by the lender. Borrowers should carefully consider the cost of borrowing and the potential return on investment before opting for a bridge loan.

Bridge loans are beneficial in various scenarios.

1. For **individuals who have found their dream home** but have yet to sell their current property, a bridge loan can provide the necessary funds to secure the new property. This eliminates the need for a contingent offer, making the buyer's offer more attractive to sellers.
2. **Real estate investors** who aim to capitalize on time-sensitive investment opportunities can use bridge loans to quickly acquire properties, renovate them, and increase their value before securing long-term financing or selling the property for a profit.

In summary, bridge loans serve as temporary financing solutions that bridge the gap during property transitions. They provide immediate funding to individuals or investors who need liquidity while awaiting the sale of a property or securing long-term financing. Bridge loans offer a faster and more flexible alternative to traditional financing options, although they come with higher interest rates and shorter repayment terms.

2.5 Home Equity Loans: Unlocking the Value of Your Home

Home equity loans provide property owners with a means to tap into the equity they have accumulated in their properties. This section explores how home equity loans work, the potential uses for the funds, and the considerations borrowers should keep in mind, such as interest rates and repayment terms.

A home equity loan allows property owners to borrow against the **equity they have built in their homes** over time. Equity represents the difference between the market value of the property and the outstanding balance on the mortgage. As property owners make mortgage payments and the value of their property appreciates, their equity increases, providing an asset that can be utilized through a home equity loan.

Home equity loans typically come in two forms: traditional home equity loans and home equity lines of credit (HELOCs).

1. With a **traditional home equity loan**, borrowers receive a lump sum of money, which they repay over a fixed term with a fixed interest rate.
2. On the other hand, a HELOC offers borrowers a **revolving line of credit**, similar to a credit card, from which they can *draw funds as needed* during a specified draw period, typically 5 to 10 years.

Both types of home equity loans allow borrowers to **tap into their home's equity**, but they differ in *terms of repayment stru*cture and flexibility.

The funds from a home equity loan can be used for various purposes. Many property owners opt to use home equity loans to *finance home improvements* or renovations, which can increase the value of their property. Others may use the funds for *educational expenses, debt consolidation, medical bills*, or other major expenses. The versatility of home equity loans allows borrowers to leverage the value of their property to meet their financial needs.

Interest rates on home equity loans are typically lower than other types of loans, such as personal loans or credit cards since they are secured by the property. However, the interest rates on home equity loans are generally higher than those on primary mortgage loans. The exact interest rate offered to borrowers depends on factors such as *creditworthiness, loan amount, loan-to-value ratio*, and *current market conditions*. Borrowers should carefully evaluate the interest rates and terms offered by various lenders to ensure they secure the most favorable option.

Repayment terms for home equity loans vary depending on the lender and the borrower's preferences.

1. **Traditional home equity loans** often feature fixed interest rates and fixed repayment terms, typically ranging from 5 to 30 years. This structure provides borrowers with predictable monthly payments over the life of the loan.
2. **HELOCs**, on the other hand, often have a draw period during which borrowers can access funds and a subsequent repayment period during which they must repay the principal and interest. It's important for borrowers to understand the repayment terms, including any potential changes in interest rates or payment requirements, to effectively manage their finances.

When considering a home equity loan, borrowers should be mindful of their ability to repay the loan and the **potential risks involved**. Since home equity loans are secured by the property, failure to repay the loan could result in the loss of the home through foreclosure. It's crucial for borrowers to carefully assess their financial situation, consider the affordability of the loan payments, and have a plan in place for repayment.

In conclusion, home equity loans provide property owners with a means to access the value they have built in their properties. Whether through a traditional home equity loan or a HELOC, borrowers can use the funds for various purposes. However, borrowers should be diligent in evaluating the terms, including interest rates and repayment structures, and assess their ability to repay the loan to mitigate potential risks. By leveraging the equity in their property, property ownerss can unlock financial opportunities and meet their goals while keeping their homes as valuable assets.

2.6 Partnerships: Collaborative Real Estate Financing

Partnerships are a popular form of real estate financing that allows individuals to pool their resources and invest in real estate collectively. This section delves into the concept of partnerships as a means of real estate financing, discussing various partnership structures, profit-sharing arrangements, and the significance of defining roles and responsibilities.

A partnership in the context of real estate involves two or more individuals coming together to **jointly invest in properties**. By pooling their financial resources, expertise, and networks, partners can access larger investment opportunities and share the risks and rewards associated with real estate investments. Partnerships can take different forms, such as general partnerships or limited partnerships, each with its own legal and financial implications.

1. In a **general partnership**, all partners have equal rights and responsibilities in managing the real estate investment. Decisions are typically made collectively, and each partner is personally liable for the partnership's debts and obligations.
2. On the other hand, **limited partnerships** consist of general partners who manage the investment and limited partners who contribute capital but have limited liability. Limited partners enjoy the benefit of limited personal liability, shielding their personal assets from the partnership's liabilities.

One crucial aspect of partnerships is establishing **clear profit-sharing arrangements**. Partnerships can distribute profits in various ways, such as equal shares, based on the percentage of capital contributed, or according to a predetermined formula. It is essential for partners to define the profit-sharing structure at the outset to ensure transparency and avoid conflicts in the future. Clear agreements on profit distribution can help maintain a harmonious and productive partnership.

Defining **roles and responsibilities** is another key element in forming a successful real estate partnership. Partners should clearly delineate each member's roles, such as property management, financial management, or sourcing new investment opportunities. This clarity ensures that everyone understands their responsibilities and avoids overlapping or gaps in tasks. Regular communication and accountability are essential to maintain a well-functioning partnership.

In addition to the financial benefits, partnerships can provide access to a **wider network of resources**, including lenders, contractors, and real estate professionals. Partners can leverage their collective networks to source deals, obtain favorable financing terms, or access specialized knowledge. This expanded network can give partnerships a competitive edge and increase their chances of success in the real estate market.

However, partnerships also come with potential **challenges and risks**. Disagreements among partners, differences in risk tolerance, or changes in personal circumstances can create conflicts within the partnership. It is crucial for partners to have clear communication channels, dispute-resolution mechanisms, and contingency plans in place to address potential challenges and ensure the partnership's long-term sustainability.

In summary, real estate partnerships enable individuals to collectively invest in real estate by pooling resources, skills, and networks. Partnerships provide access to larger investment opportunities, leverage complementary skills, and expand networks. Effective communication and conflict mitigation strategies are crucial to address potential challenges.

Conclusion

In conclusion, there are several key types of real estate financing. We have explored mortgage loans, which are commonly used for residential properties, and discussed the loan application process, down payments, interest rates, and different mortgage options. Hard money loans have been introduced as short-term loans for real estate investments, highlighting their higher interest rates and shorter repayment periods. Commercial loans have been discussed as specialized financing solutions for commercial properties, covering loan-to-value ratios, underwriting criteria, and repayment structures. Bridge loans have been presented as temporary loans bridging financing gaps during property transitions. Home equity loans have been examined as a means to access the accumulated equity in a home. Lastly, partnerships is a iable weay toaccess funds from a financial partner.

Chapter 3: Choosing the Right Financing Option

Choice - Photo by qimono

3.1 Assessing Your Financing Needs: Understanding Factors for Real Estate Goals

When embarking on a real estate venture, whether it's purchasing a home, investing in commercial property, or expanding your real estate portfolio, it is crucial to assess your financing needs accurately. This process involves evaluating various factors that will influence your **choice of financing options,** ensuring that your real estate goals align with your financial capabilities. By understanding the key factors such as property type, purchase price, desired loan amount, and timeline, you can make informed decisions that pave the way for a successful venture.

The first factor to consider when assessing your financing needs is the **type of property** you are targeting. Residential properties, commercial buildings, and land acquisitions all require different financing approaches.

1. **Residential properties** often have more flexible financing options, including conventional mortgages, FHA loans, or VA loans, depending on your eligibility.
2. On the other hand, **commercial properties** may require more specialized financing, such as commercial mortgages or small business loans, taking into account factors like potential rental income and commercial viability.
3. **Land acquisitions** might involve loans specifically designed for purchasing undeveloped land or construction loans if you plan to build on the property.

Another crucial consideration is the **purchase price** of the property. The purchase price not only determines the amount of financing you will require but also affects the type of loan you can secure. Traditional mortgages typically have limits based on the purchase price, and certain loan types may have specific requirements regarding down payments and interest rates. By accurately assessing your financing needs in relation to the purchase price, you can determine whether you will need additional funds for a down payment or if you qualify for specific loan programs tailored to your budget.

Determining the **desired loan amount** is also essential in assessing your financing needs. While the purchase price gives you a starting point, the loan amount takes into account factors such as your available savings, your creditworthiness, and the *loan-to-value ratio (LTV)*. The LTV ratio is the percentage of the property value that the lender is willing to finance. Lenders typically have their own limits and guidelines for LTV ratios, which can impact the loan amount you can secure. By understanding your desired loan amount, you can evaluate your eligibility for different financing options and consider ways to optimize your financial position.

Timeline is yet another crucial factor in assessing financing needs for real estate goals. If you have a shorter timeline, you may need financing options with faster approval and processing times, such as bridge loans or hard money loans. These types of loans are designed for shorter-term financing needs and provide quick access to funds, albeit at higher interest rates. Conversely, if you have a longer timeline, you may have the flexibility to pursue traditional mortgage options, allowing for more favorable terms and lower interest rates.

By considering these factors—property type, purchase price, desired loan amount, and timeline—you can assess your financing needs effectively. This assessment allows you to narrow down the available financing options and choose the one that aligns with your real estate goals and financial capabilities. With a clear understanding of your financing needs, you can embark on your real estate venture with confidence, knowing that you have made informed decisions to support your success.

3.2 Evaluating Your Financial Situation: Determining Borrowing Capacity and Affordability

Before pursuing any financing options for your real estate goals, it is crucial to evaluate your financial situation comprehensively. This evaluation involves assessing various aspects of your financial health, including credit scores, income stability, existing debts, and financial reserves. By understanding your financial situation, you can determine your borrowing capacity and affordability, enabling you to make informed decisions about the financing options available to you.

One of the primary factors to consider when evaluating your financial situation is your **credit score**. Lenders rely on credit scores to assess your creditworthiness and determine the interest rates and loan terms they can offer you. A higher credit score generally translates to better loan terms, while a lower credit score may limit your options or result in higher interest rates. It is important to obtain a copy of your credit report from the major credit bureaus and review it for accuracy. If there are any errors or discrepancies, take steps to correct them before applying for financing. Additionally, if your credit score is lower than desired, consider implementing strategies to improve it, such as paying off outstanding debts and making timely payments.

Income stability is another critical aspect of evaluating your financial situation. Lenders assess your income to determine your ability to repay the loan. They typically consider factors such as employment history, income sources, and consistency of earnings. If you have a stable and reliable income, lenders are more likely to view you as a low-risk borrower. However, if your income is irregular or inconsistent, lenders may perceive a higher level of risk, potentially affecting the loan terms available to you. Evaluating your income stability allows you to understand how lenders may perceive your financial situation and plan accordingly.

Existing debts play a significant role in evaluating your financial situation. Lenders assess your *debt-to-income ratio (DTI)* to determine your ability to manage additional debt. Your DTI is calculated by dividing your total monthly debt payments by your gross monthly income. Lenders typically have maximum DTI limits that borrowers must meet to qualify for financing. Evaluating your existing debts and calculating your DTI helps you understand how much additional debt you can comfortably take on without straining your financial situation. It is advisable to pay down existing debts or reduce monthly obligations before applying for new financing to improve your borrowing capacity.

Financial reserves are an essential aspect to consider when evaluating your financial situation for real estate financing. Lenders often require borrowers to have sufficient reserves, such as *savings or liquid assets,* as a cushion against unexpected expenses or income disruptions. These reserves demonstrate your financial stability and ability to handle unforeseen circumstances. Evaluating your financial reserves allows you to assess whether you meet the lender's requirements or if you need to build up your savings before pursuing real estate financing. It is important to note that different loan programs and lenders may have varying reserve requirements, so it is essential to research and understand the specific guidelines applicable to your situation.

By thoroughly evaluating your financial situation, considering factors such as credit scores, income stability, existing debts, and financial reserves, you can determine your borrowing capacity and affordability. Armed with a clear understanding of your financial situation, you can approach the financing process confidently and make informed decisions that align with your real estate goals.

3.3 Comparing Financing Options: Making Informed Decisions

When it comes to financing your real estate goals, it's crucial to explore and compare the various financing options available to you. Each option has its own set of advantages and disadvantages, and understanding the key factors will allow you to make an informed decision that aligns with your financial needs and goals. In this section, we will provide a comprehensive comparison of different financing options to help you navigate the landscape effectively.

One of the primary factors to consider when comparing financing options is the **interest rate.** The interest rate directly impacts the overall cost of borrowing and determines the amount of interest you will pay over the life of the loan. Traditional mortgages typically offer lower interest rates, making them a popular choice for borrowers with good credit and stable income. Government-backed loan programs, such as FHA or VA loans, may provide more lenient eligibility requirements and competitive interest rates. On the other hand, alternative financing options like hard money loans or private financing tend to have higher interest rates due to the increased risk for the lender. By comparing interest rates across different financing options, you can assess the long-term affordability of each option.

Repayment terms are another crucial aspect to consider when comparing financing options. Repayment terms determine the duration of the loan and the frequency of payments. Traditional mortgages usually have longer repayment terms, such as 15 or 30 years, allowing borrowers to spread out their payments over a more extended period. Shorter-term loans, such as bridge loans or construction loans, often have more condensed repayment terms and may require balloon payments or refinancing at the end of the term. By evaluating the repayment terms, you can determine which option best aligns with your financial situation and real estate goals.

Fees associated with each financing option should also be taken into account. Lenders may charge various fees, including origination fees, application fees, appraisal fees, and closing costs. These fees can significantly impact the total cost of the loan and the funds you need to bring to the closing table. It is essential to review the fee structures of different financing options and compare them to ensure you understand the total cost involved. Some loan programs may offer lower upfront fees but higher interest rates, while others may have higher fees but lower interest rates. By carefully evaluating the fees, you can make a more accurate comparison and determine which option provides the most favorable cost structure for your needs.

Eligibility requirements are a critical consideration when comparing financing options. Different loan programs have different criteria regarding credit scores, income stability, down payment requirements, and property types. Traditional mortgages often have stricter eligibility requirements, such as higher credit scores and lower debt-to-income ratios. Government-backed loan programs, on the other hand, may provide more flexible eligibility criteria, making homeownership more accessible for individuals with lower credit scores or limited down payment funds. Alternative financing options like hard money loans may have more relaxed eligibility requirements but come with higher interest rates and shorter repayment terms. By comparing the eligibility requirements, you can determine which financing options you are most likely to qualify for and focus your efforts accordingly.

By considering factors such as interest rates, repayment terms, fees, and eligibility requirements, you can make a comprehensive comparison of different financing options. Armed with a thorough comparison, you can confidently select the financing option that best suits your needs, allowing you to achieve your real estate goals effectively.

3.4 Understanding Interest Rates and Terms: Key Factors in Financing

Interest rates and loan terms are essential elements to consider when assessing financing options for your real estate goals. These factors play a significant role in determining the overall cost of financing and can have a long-term impact on your financial health. In this section, we will delve into the intricacies of interest rates and terms, discussing concepts such as fixed versus variable interest rates, loan durations, prepayment penalties, and the potential risks associated with interest rate fluctuations.

One of the fundamental aspects of interest rates to understand is the distinction between fixed and variable rates.

1. **A fixed interest rate** remains constant throughout the life of the loan, providing borrowers with predictable monthly payments. This stability can be advantageous in budgeting and long-term financial planning
2. On the other hand, **variable interest rates**, also known as adjustable rates, are subject to change based on market conditions. These rates are typically tied to an index, such as the prime rate or the Secured Overnight Financing Rate (SOFR), and may fluctuate periodically. While variable rates can initially be lower than fixed rates, they introduce the potential for increased payments in the future.

Understanding the pros and cons of fixed versus variable interest rates allows you to choose the option that aligns with your risk tolerance and financial objectives.

Loan duration, often referred to as the term, is another crucial factor in understanding financing options. The term of the loan determines the length of time over which you will be making payments. Traditional mortgages typically offer terms of 15 or 30 years, although other options with shorter terms may be available. Longer loan terms generally result in *lower monthly payments* but higher overall interest costs over the life of the loan. Shorter loan terms often have *higher monthly payments* but allow borrowers to pay off the loan faster and accumulate less interest. By assessing your financial situation and long-term goals, you can determine the most suitable loan duration for your needs.

Prepayment penalties are a consideration that borrowers should be aware of when evaluating financing options. Some loans impose penalties if the borrower pays off the loan early or makes additional principal payments beyond the scheduled amounts. Prepayment penalties can significantly impact the total cost of financing and limit borrowers' flexibility to pay off their loans ahead of schedule. It is essential to review the terms and conditions of each financing option to understand if prepayment penalties apply and how they might affect your ability to save on interest costs or refinance in the future.

It is also crucial to be aware of the **potential risks** associated with interest rate fluctuations. Variable interest rates are particularly susceptible to changes in market conditions, which can lead to increased monthly payments and higher overall interest costs. If you choose a variable rate option, it is essential to understand the specific terms, such as rate adjustment periods and rate caps, to assess the potential risks involved. Additionally, even with fixed-rate loans, it is important to consider potential future refinancing needs and the potential impact of changing interest rate environments. Monitoring interest rate trends and staying informed about market conditions can help you make informed decisions and mitigate potential risks.

By understanding the intricacies of interest rates and terms, including fixed versus variable rates, loan durations, prepayment penalties, and potential risks associated with interest rate fluctuations, you can make informed decisions regarding your financing options.

3.5 Working with a Lender: Navigating the Financing Process

When it comes to securing financing for your real estate goals, establishing a productive relationship with a lender is essential. Working effectively with lenders can help streamline the financing process, ensure a smooth transaction, and increase your chances of obtaining favorable loan terms. In this section, we will provide guidance on how to navigate the financing process, including tips on finding reputable lenders, preparing necessary documentation, negotiating terms, and understanding the loan approval and closing processes.

The first step in working with a lender is to **find reputable lenders**. Research and identify lenders with a *strong track record, positive customer reviews*, and a *good reputation* in the industry. Consider seeking recommendations from trusted sources, such as real estate professionals, friends, or family members who have recently gone through the financing process. Take the time to compare the offerings, interest rates, and terms of different lenders to ensure you find one that aligns with your needs and goals.

Once you have chosen a lender, it is important to **prepare the necessary documentation**. Lenders require various documents to assess your eligibility and determine the loan amount you qualify for. Common documents include proof of income, tax returns, bank statements, employment verification, and information about the property you are financing. Organize and compile these documents in advance to expedite the loan application process. If you have any questions or uncertainties regarding the required documentation, don't hesitate to reach out to your lender for clarification.

When it comes to negotiating loan terms, **effective communication** is key. Clearly articulate your financial goals, preferences, and concerns to your lender. Discuss aspects such as interest rates, loan durations, fees, and any specific requirements you may have. Be open to exploring different options and ask questions to ensure you fully understand the terms and implications of each. Remember that negotiation is a two-way process, and both parties should feel comfortable with the final terms. Seek professional advice from *mortgage brokers* or *financial advisors* if you need assistance in understanding or negotiating the terms.

Understanding the **loan approval and closing processes** is crucial for a smooth transaction. Your lender will evaluate your application, review the documentation you provide, and assess your creditworthiness and financial stability. This evaluation process may involve additional requests for information or documentation. Once your loan is approved, you will enter the closing process, where the final paperwork is prepared, and the funds are disbursed. Familiarize yourself with the timelines and steps involved in these processes, and stay in close communication with your lender to ensure a timely and successful closing.

Throughout the financing process, maintaining **clear and open communication** with your lender is paramount. Promptly respond to any requests for information or documentation, and keep your lender updated on any changes to your financial situation. If any issues or concerns arise during the process, address them promptly with your lender to find suitable resolutions. Remember that your lender is a valuable resource and can provide guidance and support throughout the financing journey.

Working effectively with a lender requires diligence, preparation, and clear communication. Find reputable lenders, organize the necessary documentation, negotiate terms that align with your goals, and seek professional advice when needed. Understand the loan approval and closing processes to ensure a successful transaction.

Conclusion

In summary, choosing the right financing option requires a comprehensive assessment of your needs, a thorough evaluation of your financial situation, and a comparison of available options. Carefully consider interest rates, terms, and lender relationships to ensure you make the best decision for your real estate financing needs. By doing so, you can set yourself up for success in achieving your real estate goals.

Chapter 4: Preparing for Real Estate Financing

Save - Photo by Towfiqu barbhuiya

4.1 Understanding the Crucial Role of Credit Scores in Real Estate Financing

In the realm of real estate financing, few things carry as much weight as an individual's credit score. A credit score is a numerical representation of an individual's creditworthiness, indicating their ability to handle financial obligations responsibly. This section aims to shed light on the significance of credit scores in the real estate financing process, explaining how they are calculated, the factors that influence them, and why maintaining a good credit score is vital for securing favorable financing terms. Additionally, it offers valuable tips on improving credit scores and maintaining a healthy credit history.

Credit scores are typically calculated using complex algorithms that consider various factors, including payment history, credit utilization, length of credit history, credit mix, and new credit applications.

Payment history, for instance, accounts for a significant portion of the credit score calculation, reflecting whether an individual has made timely payments on their credit accounts. Credit utilization, which measures the percentage of available credit being used, is another crucial factor that can impact credit scores. The length of credit history, credit mix, and new credit applications also play a role in determining creditworthiness.

A good credit score is crucial when it comes to obtaining favorable financing terms for real estate investments. Lenders use credit scores to assess the risk associated with lending money to individuals. A higher credit score signifies a lower risk, which often translates into lower interest rates, more flexible loan terms, and a higher likelihood of loan approval. With a good credit score, borrowers are more likely to secure mortgages with lower interest rates, reducing the overall cost of borrowing and potentially saving thousands of dollars over the life of the loan. Additionally, a good credit score can also enhance one's ability to negotiate better terms when refinancing existing mortgages.

Improving and maintaining a good credit score requires diligence and responsible financial management. Here are some valuable tips to help individuals **enhance their creditworthiness**:

1. **Pay bills on time:** Timely payment of all financial obligations is crucial for a healthy credit history. Consider setting up automatic payments or reminders to ensure payments are made promptly.
2. **Manage credit utilization:** Aim to keep credit card balances low and avoid maxing out credit limits. Ideally, strive to utilize less than 30% of available credit.
3. **Monitor credit reports:** Regularly review credit reports to identify errors or fraudulent activity. Reporting any inaccuracies promptly can help maintain an accurate credit

profile.

4. **Avoid unnecessary credit applications:** Excessive credit applications within a short period can negatively impact credit scores. Apply for credit sparingly and only when necessary.
5. **Establish a credit history: If** starting with limited credit history, consider obtaining a secured credit card or becoming an authorized user on someone else's account to establish and build credit.
6. **Maintain a diverse credit mix:** A healthy credit mix, including a combination of credit cards, loans, and mortgages, can demonstrate responsible credit management.

Understanding the significance of credit scores in the real estate financing process is paramount for aspiring homeowners and investors. By comprehending how credit scores are calculated, the factors that influence

4.2 Saving for a Down Payment:

When it comes to real estate financing, saving for a down payment plays a pivotal role. A down payment is a significant upfront payment made by the buyer, representing a percentage of the total purchase price. This section emphasizes the importance of saving for a down payment, offers strategies for effective money-saving, explores different down payment requirements for various loan programs, and highlights the advantages of a larger down payment, such as lower interest rates and reduced loan-to-value ratios.

The Significance of Saving for a Down Payment

Saving for a down payment is essential for several reasons.

1. Firstly, it demonstrates *financial responsibility* and discipline to lenders, indicating an individual's ability to manage and save money.
2. Additionally, a *larger down payment* can significantly impact the terms of the mortgage loan, including interest rates, loan-to-value ratios, and monthly payments.

By having a substantial down payment, borrowers can potentially secure more favorable financing terms and save money in the long run.

Strategies for Saving Money

Saving for a down payment requires careful planning and disciplined financial habits. Here are some effective strategies to help individuals save money:

1. *Establish a budget:* Create a realistic budget that allows for savings by tracking income, and expenses, and identifying areas where costs can be reduced.
2. *Cut unnecessary expenses:* Analyze monthly expenses and identify areas where spending can be trimmed. This might include dining out less frequently, reducing entertainment expenses, or finding more affordable alternatives for everyday items.
3. *Set up automatic transfers:* Arrange for a portion of each paycheck to be automatically transferred to a separate savings account dedicated to the down payment. This ensures consistent savings without relying on willpower alone.
4. *Explore additional income sources:* Consider taking on a side job or freelance work to generate extra income specifically earmarked for the down payment.
5. *Downsize temporarily:* Evaluate the possibility of downsizing

living arrangements or finding more affordable housing options temporarily to accelerate savings.

Down Payment Requirements for Loan Programs

Different loan programs have varying down payment requirements, and understanding these requirements is crucial when planning for real estate financing.

1. **Conventional loans** typically require a down payment of 10% to 20% of the purchase price.
2. **Government-backed loan programs**, such as FHA loans, often have more lenient down payment requirements, allowing borrowers to put down as little as 3.5% of the purchase price.
3. Veterans and active-duty military personnel may qualify for **VA loans**, which often require *no down payment* at all.

Researching and understanding the options available can help borrowers determine the most suitable loan program and down payment amount for their financial situation.

Advantages of a Larger Down Payment

Saving for a larger down payment offers several advantages when seeking real estate financing.

1. Firstly, a larger down payment **reduces the loan-to-value ratio**, which is the proportion of the loan amount compared to the property's appraised value. A lower loan-to-value ratio decreases the lender's risk, potentially leading to more favorable interest rates and loan terms.
2. Secondly, a larger down payment can result in **lower**

monthly mortgage payments, providing financial flexibility and potentially freeing up funds for other purposes.
3. Moreover, a substantial down payment can **contribute to the borrower's equity** in the property from the start, providing a stronger financial position and potential for future property value appreciation.

Saving for a down payment is a critical aspect of real estate financing. By prioritizing savings and adopting effective money-saving strategies, individuals can accumulate the necessary funds to secure a substantial down payment. Understanding the down payment requirements for different loan programs and recognizing the advantages of a larger down payment can empower borrowers to make informed decisions, potentially leading to more favorable financing terms, reduced interest rates, and increased financial stability in their real estate endeavors.

4.3 Organizing Your Finances:

When seeking real estate financing, it is crucial to present a favorable financial profile to lenders. This section provides valuable guidance on organizing personal finances to demonstrate financial responsibility and stability. It covers essential topics such as managing debts, creating a budget, and improving financial stability. By following these guidelines, individuals can enhance their chances of securing favorable financing terms and achieving their real estate goals.

Managing Debts

One of the key aspects of organizing personal finances is effectively managing debts. Lenders closely evaluate an individual's debt-to-income ratio (DTI), which compares the amount of debt owed to the income earned. To maintain a healthy DTI, it is important to:

1. **Pay off high-interest debts:** Prioritize paying off debts with high interest rates, such as credit card balances, as they can significantly impact your financial profile and ability to obtain favorable financing terms.
2. **Consolidate debts:** Consider consolidating multiple debts into a single loan or credit line with a lower interest rate. This can simplify payments and potentially reduce monthly obligations.
3. **Avoid taking on new debts:** Minimize new debt obligations, such as financing large purchases or applying for new credit cards, as it can increase the DTI and raise concerns for lenders.

Creating a Budget

Creating a comprehensive budget is an essential step towards financial organization. A budget helps individuals track their income and expenses, allowing them to allocate funds wisely and make informed financial decisions. When creating a budget:

1. **Identify income sources:** Determine all sources of income, including salaries, investments, and any other additional income streams.
2. **Track expenses:** Closely monitor and categorize all expenses, including fixed expenses (rent, utilities) and variable expenses (groceries, entertainment). This provides clarity on spending habits and areas where adjustments can be made.
3. **Set savings goals:** Allocate a portion of your income towards savings, including a dedicated fund for the down payment. This ensures consistent progress towards financial goals.

Improving Financial Stability

Demonstrating financial stability is vital when seeking real estate financing. Lenders assess an individual's financial stability based on factors such as income stability, employment history, and savings. To improve financial stability:

1. **Maintain a stable income:** Consistency in income is crucial, as lenders prefer borrowers with steady employment. Avoid frequent job changes unless necessary and strive for career growth and advancement.
2. **Build an emergency fund:** Establish an emergency fund that can cover at least three to six months of living expenses. This demonstrates preparedness and financial stability to lenders.
3. **Save for retirement:** Contributing to retirement accounts showcases long-term financial planning and stability, reinforcing your financial profile.
4. **Review insurance coverage:** Adequate insurance coverage, such as health, home, and life insurance, provides protection against unforeseen events and enhances financial stability.

Organizing personal finances is an essential step in presenting a favorable financial profile to lenders when seeking real estate financing. By effectively managing debts, creating a budget, and improving financial stability, individuals can demonstrate their financial responsibility and increase their chances of securing favorable financing terms. Taking proactive steps towards organizing personal finances not only benefits the real estate financing process but also lays a strong foundation for long-term financial well-being.

4.4 Getting Pre-approved for a Loan:

Before embarking on a real estate search, it is highly advantageous to get pre-approved for a loan. This section highlights the benefits of obtaining pre-approval, explaining the pre-approval process, including submitting an application, providing documentation, and undergoing a credit check. By understanding the significance of pre-approval, individuals can enhance their credibility, streamline the homebuying process, and make more competitive offers.

The Benefits of Pre-approval

Obtaining pre-approval for a loan offers several advantages for prospective homebuyers. These benefits include:

1. **Enhanced credibility:** Pre-approval demonstrates to sellers that you are a serious and *qualified buyer*. It reassures them that you have undergone a thorough financial assessment by a lender, increasing your credibility in a competitive real estate market.
2. **Clear budget and price range:** Through pre-approval, you gain clarity on your budget and price range. Lenders evaluate your financial situation, considering factors such as income, credit history, and debt-to-income ratio. This assessment allows you to focus on properties within your means, saving time and effort in the home search.
3. **Competitive advantage:** Pre-approval provides a competitive edge in a seller's market. It enables you to submit offers with confidence, knowing that you have already secured financing. Sellers are more likely to consider and favor offers from pre-approved buyers, as it reduces the risk of the deal falling through due to financing issues.

Using Pre-approval to Your Advantage

After obtaining pre-approval, you can leverage this advantage in various ways during the home buying process:

1. **Targeted search:** With a clear budget and price range, you can focus your search on properties that align with your financial capabilities. This saves time and avoids disappointment from falling in love with a home that may be outside your price range.
2. **Negotiation power:** Pre-approval gives you the confidence to negotiate with sellers. It shows that you are a qualified buyer with financing in place, making your offer more attractive and potentially strengthening your bargaining position.
3. **Faster closing process:** Pre-approval streamlines the closing process. Since much of the financial groundwork has already been completed, the time between offer acceptance and closing can be significantly reduced.

Getting pre-approved for a loan is a crucial step in the real estate financing process. By understanding the benefits of pre-approval, individuals can strengthen their credibility, establish a clear budget, and gain a competitive advantage in the market.

Conclusion

To summarize, successful real estate financing requires careful preparation and organization. Key factors highlighted in this chapter include maintaining a good credit score, saving for a down payment, organizing personal finances, and getting pre-approved for a loan. By focusing on these aspects and applying the knowledge provided, readers can confidently navigate the financing process, make informed decisions, and set themselves up for success in their real estate endeavors.

Chapter 5: Real Estate Financing Process

Process Steps - Photo by geralt

5.1 Finding the Right Property

Finding the right property is an essential initial step in the real estate financing process. This section will guide you through the process of identifying a property that meets your requirements, aligns with your budget, and supports your financing goals. By defining your needs, conducting thorough property searches, and leveraging the expertise of real estate professionals, you can increase your chances of finding the perfect property for your real estate investment.

Defining Your Requirements

Before embarking on your property search, it is crucial to define your requirements. Consider factors such as *location*, *property type*, *size*, *amenities*, and proximity to essential services. Determine your must-haves and prioritize them accordingly. This will help narrow down your search and ensure that the properties you explore align with your specific needs and preferences.

Conducting Property Searches

With your requirements in mind, begin your property search using various resources. Online *real estate platforms*, *local listings*, and *real estate agent networks* are valuable sources of property information. Leverage advanced search filters to refine your results based on your desired criteria, such as price range, number of bedrooms, and specific neighborhood.

It is also beneficial to explore different neighborhoods and areas to gain a comprehensive understanding of the *local real estate market*. Take note of property prices, market trends, and potential growth opportunities. Additionally, consider attending open houses or scheduling property viewings to get a firsthand look at the properties that pique your interest.

Working with Real Estate Professionals

Collaborating with experienced real estate agents or brokers can significantly streamline your property search. These professionals have *in-depth knowledge* of the local market, access to exclusive listings, and expertise in negotiating real estate transactions.

When selecting a real estate professional, ensure they understand your financing goals and have experience working with buyers in a similar financial situation. Communicate your requirements and budget clearly, and establish open lines of communication to facilitate a smooth property search process.

Real estate agents can provide *valuable insights*, offer guidance on *market conditions*, assist with *property comparisons*, and help you navigate the financing aspects of the purchasing process. They can also refer you to trusted mortgage lenders or professionals who specialize in real estate financing, further streamlining the overall process.

In summary, finding the right property is a critical step in real estate financing. Defining your requirements, conducting thorough searches, and collaborating with experienced professionals can enhance your chances of identifying a property that aligns with your goals and budget. It's important to remain flexible, conduct diligent research, consider multiple options, and seek guidance from experts. When you find the right property, you can proceed with confidence, knowing that it is a suitable investment that aligns with your financial objectives.

5.2 Applying for Financing: Navigating the Real Estate Financing Application Process

Applying for financing is a crucial step in the real estate financing process. This section will guide you through the necessary steps to complete a loan application, provide the required financial documentation, and submit your application to lenders. By understanding the application process and ensuring accuracy and thoroughness, you can maximize your chances of securing the financing needed for your real estate investment.

Completing the Loan Application

The loan application is a *formal document* that provides lenders with essential information about your financial situation and the property you intend to purchase. When completing the application, pay careful attention to accuracy and thoroughness. Provide *detailed and up-to-date information*, including personal details, employment history, income, and assets. Be prepared to disclose any debts or liabilities you may have.

To simplify the application process, gather all necessary documents beforehand, such as identification, tax returns, pay stubs, bank statements, and any additional financial records required by the lender. Having these documents readily available will help ensure a smooth and efficient application submission.

Providing Financial Documentation

Lenders require various financial documents to assess your creditworthiness and determine the loan terms. Commonly requested documents include:

1. *Proof of Income:* This includes recent pay stubs, W-2 forms, and tax returns. Self-employed individuals may need to provide additional documentation, such as profit and loss statements or 1099 forms.
2. *Bank Statements:* Lenders typically request several months of bank statements to verify your financial stability and analyze your spending habits. Make sure to provide complete and accurate statements for all relevant accounts.
3. *Asset Documentation:* If you have assets such as investments, real estate properties, or retirement accounts, you may need to provide supporting documentation, such as statements or legal agreements.
4. *Debt Information:* Provide detailed information about any outstanding debts, including credit card balances, student loans, auto loans, or other liabilities. Include account numbers, balances, and monthly payment amounts.

Submitting the Application

Once you have completed the loan application and gathered all the required financial documentation, it is time to submit your application to lenders. You can choose to submit applications to multiple lenders simultaneously to compare loan offers and increase your chances of securing favorable financing terms.

It is important to note that during the application process, lenders will *conduct a credit check* to assess your creditworthiness. This check may temporarily impact your credit score. However, multiple credit checks conducted within a short period for the purpose of mortgage applications are typically treated as a single inquiry, minimizing the impact on your credit score.

In summary, applying for real estate financing requires careful attention to detail and thoroughness. Completing the loan application accurately, providing necessary documentation, and submitting to multiple lenders improves your chances of securing favorable financing terms. Maintain open communication with lenders, promptly respond to requests, and stay informed about your application's progress. By being proactive and organized, you can navigate the financing application process smoothly and move closer to achieving your real estate goals.

5.3 Underwriting and Approval Process: Evaluating Loan Applications for Real Estate Financing

The underwriting and approval process is a crucial stage in real estate financing. After submitting your loan application, lenders meticulously evaluate your financial and creditworthiness, assess the property's value and condition, and determine the terms and conditions of the loan. This section will provide insights into the underwriting process, highlighting the factors that influence loan approval and the potential requirements borrowers may encounter.

Assessing Financial and Creditworthiness

During the underwriting process, lenders thoroughly review your financial information to determine your *creditworthiness*. This includes examining your income, employment history, debt-to-income ratio, credit score, and credit history. They assess your ability to repay the loan based on these factors.

Lenders typically request additional documentation during underwriting, such as updated bank statements, employment verification, and explanations for any significant financial events or discrepancies. It is crucial to respond promptly and provide the requested information to ensure a smooth underwriting process.

Evaluating Property Value and Condition

In addition to assessing your financial profile, lenders also evaluate the property being financed. This involves obtaining an *appraisal* to determine the property's current market value. The appraisal ensures that the loan amount does not exceed the property's worth, minimizing the lender's risk.

Furthermore, lenders may require a property *inspection* to assess its condition. This is particularly important for certain loan programs or properties in need of repairs. The inspection helps determine if the property meets the lender's standards and if any additional requirements or conditions need to be met before finalizing the loan.

Determining Loan Terms and Conditions

Based on the evaluation of your financial profile and the property, lenders determine the terms and conditions of the loan. This includes the *loan amount*, *interest rate*, *repayment period*, and any additional fees or requirements. The terms are influenced by factors such as credit score, loan-to-value ratio, debt-to-income ratio, and the property's condition.

It is essential to carefully review the loan offer and consider the implications of the terms and conditions. Seek clarification from the lender if needed and compare offers from multiple lenders to ensure you secure the most favorable financing terms for your real estate investment.

Loan Approval and Closing

Upon completing the underwriting process and meeting all requirements, the lender will issue a loan approval, subject to certain conditions. These conditions may include providing *additional documentation*, securing *insurance coverage*, or addressing any outstanding issues related to the property or borrower's financial situation.

Once all conditions are satisfied, the loan will move toward closing. This involves

1. signing the loan documents,
2. transferring the funds, and
3. finalizing the real estate transaction.

The closing process typically involves various parties, including the borrower, lender, real estate agents, and legal professionals.

In summary, the underwriting and approval process plays a crucial role in real estate financing. Lenders evaluate the borrower's financial and creditworthiness, property value, and loan terms. To enhance approval chances and secure favorable terms, borrowers should understand underwriting factors, meet lender requirements, and maintain proactive communication. Responding promptly to requests and collaborating closely with the lender ensures a smooth journey toward successful loan approval and closing.

5.4 Closing the Deal: Finalizing the Real Estate Financing Process

The closing of a real estate deal is the culmination of the financing process. In this section, we will explore the final stages leading up to the closing, including property appraisals, inspections, title searches, and the coordination of documents and funds. Thorough due diligence and effective communication are essential during this phase to ensure a smooth and successful closing.

Property Appraisal and Inspections

Before closing the deal, a property appraisal is typically conducted to determine its *market value*. The appraisal helps ensure that the loan amount aligns with the property's worth and protects both the buyer and the lender from overpaying. Additionally, inspections may be conducted to assess the property's condition and identify any potential issues that could impact its value or the buyer's decision to proceed with the purchase. These inspections may cover areas such as structural integrity, plumbing, electrical systems, and more.

Title Search and Insurance

A title search is essential to verify the property's ownership history and ensure that there are *no liens*, *encumbrances*, or *legal disputes* associated with it. This step helps establish a clear title for the buyer, giving them peace of mind. Title insurance is often obtained to protect against any undiscovered issues that may arise after the purchase. It is crucial to work with a qualified title company or attorney to conduct a comprehensive title search and secure appropriate title insurance.

Document Preparation and Review:

During the closing process, various legal and financial documents must be prepared, reviewed, and signed by the buyer, seller, and lender. These documents may include the *purchase agreement*, *loan documents*, *property transfer deeds*, *disclosure statements*, and any other required legal paperwork. It is vital for all parties involved to carefully review the documents, seek clarification if needed, and ensure accuracy before signing.

Coordinating Funds and Closing Costs

Closing costs, including fees for appraisals, inspections, title searches, insurance, and other services, must be accounted for and paid. The buyer and seller will coordinate the *transfer of funds* through the appropriate channels, such as wire transfers or certified checks. It is crucial to understand the breakdown of closing costs and have the necessary funds available to cover them.

Effective Communication and Coordination

Throughout the closing process, effective communication and coordination among all parties involved are paramount. This includes the buyer, seller, real estate agents, lenders, title company or attorney, and any other professionals involved in the transaction. Regular updates, prompt responses to inquiries, and adherence to timelines are essential to ensure a smooth closing.

In summary, closing the deal is the final stage of real estate financing, and careful attention to detail is crucial. Conducting appraisals, inspections, and title searches, coordinating documents and funds, and maintaining communication are essential for a successful closing. Thorough due diligence and collaboration with professionals contribute to a smooth process and the achievement of investment goals.

5.5 Repaying Your Loan: Managing Financial Obligations in Real Estate Financing

Repaying your loan is a crucial aspect of the real estate financing process. In this section, we will explore various repayment options and discuss the importance of creating a repayment plan, budgeting for loan payments, and managing your financial obligations to ensure timely and successful loan repayment.

Understanding Repayment Options

When it comes to repaying your real estate loan, you will typically have several options.

1. The most common repayment method is through monthly installments, where you make fixed payments that include

both *principal and interest portions.*

2. Another option is *interest-only payments*, where you initially pay only the interest for a specified period, and then transition into principal and interest payments.
3. Additionally, some loans may have *balloon payments*, requiring a larger final payment at the end of the loan term.

It is crucial to understand the repayment options associated with your specific loan and plan accordingly.

Creating a Repayment Plan

To ensure a smooth loan repayment process, it is essential to create a repayment plan that *aligns with your financial goals* and capabilities. Start by analyzing your budget and determining how much you can comfortably allocate towards loan payments each month. Consider factors such as your income, other financial obligations, and long-term financial objectives. With a well-defined repayment plan, you can better manage your finances and stay on track with your loan obligations.

Budgeting for Loan Payments

Budgeting plays a vital role in successfully repaying your loan. Allocate a portion of your monthly income specifically for loan payments. Ensure that your budget accounts for not only the principal and interest payments but also additional costs such as *property taxes, homeowner's insurance*, and any *escrow accounts*. By prioritizing loan payments within your budget, you can avoid financial strain and maintain a healthy financial position.

Managing Financial Obligations

Maintaining good financial health is crucial during the loan repayment phase. Make *timely payments* to avoid late fees and penalties that could impact your credit score. Stay organized by keeping track of payment due dates and setting up reminders to ensure you never miss a payment. If you encounter financial difficulties, communicate with your lender promptly to explore potential solutions such as loan modifications or repayment plans.

Avoiding Default

Defaulting on your loan should be avoided at all costs. Default occurs when you fail to make payments as agreed upon in the loan agreement. This can have severe consequences, including *damage to your credit score*, *foreclosure*, and *potential legal actions*. By prioritizing loan payments, budgeting effectively, and managing your financial obligations responsibly, you can significantly reduce the risk of default and protect your financial well-being.

In summary, repaying your real estate loan is a vital responsibility in the financing process. Understanding repayment options, creating a plan, budgeting for payments, and managing financial obligations responsibly are key. Stay proactive, monitor finances closely, and communicate with your lender if challenges arise. With careful planning and financial management, you can fulfill loan obligations and pave the way for a secure and successful real estate investment journey.

Conclusion

In conclusion, the real estate financing process requires careful consideration and proactive actions. Finding the right property, applying for financing accurately, navigating the underwriting process, closing the deal with attention to detail, and managing loan repayment are all crucial steps. Understanding credit scores, organizing finances, and maintaining a good credit history are key factors for securing favorable loan terms. Seeking guidance from professionals and following a step-by-step approach will contribute to a successful real estate investment journey.

Chapter 6: Working with a Mortgage Broker

Mortgage Broker - Photo by RDNE Stock project

6.1 Working with a Mortgage Broker: Simplifying Real Estate Financing

In the realm of real estate financing, mortgage brokers play a vital role as intermediaries between borrowers and lenders. This section serves as an introduction to mortgage brokers, shedding light on their significance and the benefits they offer in the real estate financing process. Readers will gain a better understanding of how mortgage brokers can simplify their journey towards securing suitable loan options based on their specific needs and financial circumstances.

The Role of Mortgage Brokers

Mortgage brokers serve as independent professionals who connect borrowers with lenders. They have access to a *wide range of loan products* and financial institutions, allowing them to effectively match borrowers with suitable financing options. Mortgage brokers act as knowledgeable guides throughout the financing process, providing valuable insights and expertise to help borrowers make informed decisions.

Expert Guidance and Market Knowledge

One of the key advantages of working with a mortgage broker is their expert guidance and market knowledge. Mortgage brokers are well-versed in the intricacies of real estate financing, staying up-to-date with the latest trends, interest rates, and lending criteria. They can offer *personalized advice* tailored to the borrower's unique financial situation, helping them navigate through the complex landscape of loan options.

Access to a Wide Range of Loan Products

Mortgage brokers have access to a diverse range of loan products from various lenders, including *banks*, *credit unions*, and *private lenders*. This extensive network enables them to match borrowers with loan options that align with their financial goals, credit history, and specific requirements. By leveraging their connections, mortgage brokers can often secure more favorable terms and interest rates for borrowers.

Streamlined Application and Approval Process

Working with a mortgage broker can streamline the application and approval process. Instead of approaching multiple lenders individually, borrowers can rely on the expertise of a mortgage broker to gather the necessary documentation, submit applications, and negotiate on their behalf. This *saves time and effort*, as the mortgage broker takes care of the legwork and ensures that all the required information is properly presented to lenders.

Negotiation and Advocacy

Mortgage brokers act as advocates for borrowers throughout the financing process. They negotiate with lenders on behalf of borrowers, striving to secure the best possible terms and conditions. Mortgage brokers possess the skills and experience to present borrowers' financial profiles in the most favorable light, increasing the chances of loan approval and obtaining favorable financing terms.

In summary, mortgage brokers play a crucial role in simplifying the real estate financing process. By acting as intermediaries between borrowers and lenders, mortgage brokers offer expert guidance, market knowledge, and access to a wide range of loan products. They streamline the application and approval process, negotiate on behalf of borrowers, and work to secure the most favorable financing terms.

6.2 Finding the Right Mortgage Broker for You: Choosing a Trusted Partner

Finding the right mortgage broker is crucial to ensuring a smooth and successful real estate financing experience. In this section, we will explore the factors to consider when selecting a mortgage broker who best aligns with your needs and preferences. By conducting thorough research and evaluation, readers will gain the knowledge to choose a trusted partner who will guide them through the financing process.

Reputation and Track Record

One of the first factors to consider when selecting a mortgage broker is their reputation and track record in the industry. Look for brokers with a solid reputation for professionalism, integrity, and exceptional customer service. Reading *online reviews, seeking recommendations from trusted sources*, and *checking their track record* can provide valuable insights into their performance and reliability. A reputable mortgage broker will have a history of successfully assisting clients in securing favorable financing terms and navigating the complexities of the process.

Experience and Expertise

The experience and expertise of a mortgage broker are critical considerations. Determine *how long they have been in the industry* and their level of knowledge in real estate financing. An experienced broker will have a deep understanding of the lending landscape, including various loan products, interest rates, and lender requirements. Consider their familiarity with the specific type of financing you require, such as investment properties, or refinancing. Choose a mortgage broker who has demonstrated expertise in your specific financing needs to ensure they can effectively guide you through the process.

Licensing and Accreditation

Ensure that the mortgage broker you choose is properly licensed and accredited in your jurisdiction. Mortgage brokers are typically regulated by financial authorities, and a valid license indicates their compliance with industry standards and regulations. Verify their credentials and *confirm their standing with relevant regulatory bodies.* Working with a licensed mortgage broker provides an added layer of assurance that they adhere to professional standards and have the necessary qualifications to assist you with your financing needs.

Specialization and Connections

Consider whether the mortgage broker has specific areas of specialization that align with your requirements. For instance, if you have unique financing needs, such as self-employed individuals or non-traditional income sources, look for a broker with expertise in those areas. Specialized brokers often have established relationships with lenders who cater to specific borrower profiles, increasing the likelihood of finding suitable financing options. Additionally, a mortgage broker with a robust network of connections can offer access to a wider range of loan products and potential cost savings.

Personal Connection and Communication

The relationship between a borrower and a mortgage broker is built on trust and effective communication. When evaluating mortgage brokers, assess their ability to *listen*, *understand your needs*, and *respond promptly to your inquiries*. A good mortgage broker should take the time to explain complex concepts, guide you through the process, and keep you informed at each stage. Choose a broker with whom you feel comfortable and who prioritizes open and transparent communication, ensuring that you are well informed and confident throughout the financing journey.

Selecting the right mortgage broker is a crucial step in your real estate financing journey. By considering factors such as reputation, experience, licensing, specialization, and personal connection, you can choose a trusted partner who will provide personalized guidance and support. Thorough research and evaluation of potential mortgage brokers will empower you to make an informed decision, ensuring a positive and successful financing experience.

6.3 Working Effectively with Your Mortgage Broker:

Establishing a Productive Partnership

Once you have chosen a trusted mortgage broker to assist you with your real estate financing, it's important to establish a productive working relationship. In this section, we will provide advice on how to effectively work with your mortgage broker. By following these guidelines, you can ensure clear communication, streamline the process, and maximize the benefits of their expertise.

Open and Transparent Communication

Communication is the foundation of a successful partnership with your mortgage broker. Be proactive in sharing your financial goals, preferences, and any concerns or questions you may have. Provide accurate and complete information about your *financial situation*, including income, assets, debts, and credit history. Transparency is key to enabling your mortgage broker to find the most suitable loan options for your specific needs. *Regularly communicate* with your broker and promptly respond to their requests for additional documentation or information.

Provide Necessary Documentation

To facilitate the financing process, be prepared to provide the necessary documentation requested by your mortgage broker. This may include *income verification documents*, *bank statements*, *tax returns*, and *proof of assets*. Timely and organized submission of required documents will help expedite the underwriting and approval process. Work closely with your broker to understand the specific documentation requirements and ensure you provide them in a timely manner. This will demonstrate your commitment to the process and enhance the efficiency of the financing process.

Discuss Financial Goals and Preferences

During your initial meetings with your mortgage broker, take the time to discuss your financial goals and preferences. Clearly communicate your budget, desired loan terms, and any specific features or requirements you have in mind. Your broker can then leverage their expertise to present you with suitable loan options that align with your goals. Openly discuss any concerns or limitations you may have, such as potential changes in your financial circumstances or future plans, to ensure your broker considers them in the loan selection process.

Seek Clarification and Understanding

Real estate financing can involve complex concepts and terminology. Don't hesitate to seek clarification if there is something you do not understand. A good mortgage broker will be patient and willing to explain any aspects of the process or loan terms that may be unclear. By gaining a thorough understanding of the financing details, you can make informed decisions and feel confident about the choices you make.

Maintain Regular Communication

Throughout the financing process, maintain regular communication with your mortgage broker. Stay updated on the progress of your loan application, any potential issues or delays, and important milestones. Promptly respond to any requests or inquiries from your broker to ensure a smooth and efficient process. Regularly check in with your broker for updates and be available to discuss any necessary adjustments or decisions that may arise during the financing journey.

Working effectively with your mortgage broker is essential for a successful real estate financing experience. By maintaining open and transparent communication, providing necessary documentation in a timely manner, discussing your financial goals and preferences, and seeking clarification when needed, you can establish a productive partnership with your mortgage broker. This collaborative approach will enable your broker to leverage their expertise and guide you through the financing process, ultimately helping you secure the most suitable loan for your needs.

6.4 Case Studies: Real-Life Examples of Working with Mortgage Brokers

In this section, we present real-life case studies that highlight the value and benefits of working with mortgage brokers. These case studies illustrate how mortgage brokers can assist borrowers in securing financing and navigating complex situations. By examining these examples, readers will gain practical insights into the ways mortgage brokers can find tailored solutions to meet borrowers' specific needs.

Case Study 1: First-Time Homebuyer

Mr. and Mrs. Johnson were first-time homebuyers with limited knowledge of the real estate financing process. They were unsure about the loan options available to them and were concerned about finding affordable financing. They decided to work with a mortgage broker who specialized in assisting first-time buyers. The mortgage broker guided them through the process, explaining the various loan programs and helping them understand their eligibility. By leveraging their network of lenders, the mortgage broker presented Mr. and Mrs. Johnson with competitive loan options that aligned with their financial goals. With their mortgage broker's guidance, they secured a loan with favorable terms, including a low down payment requirement, enabling them to purchase their dream home.

Case Study 2: Self-Employed Borrower

Ms. Martinez was a self-employed business owner seeking financing to purchase a commercial property. She faced challenges in proving her income and navigating the complex documentation requirements associated with self-employment. Recognizing the unique needs of self-employed borrowers, Ms. Martinez decided to work with a mortgage broker experienced in assisting entrepreneurs. The mortgage broker helped her gather the necessary documentation, such as tax returns, profit and loss statements, and bank statements, to demonstrate her income stability and creditworthiness. With the mortgage broker's expertise, Ms. Martinez was able to secure a commercial loan with competitive rates and terms tailored to her business needs.

Case Study 3: Complex Financial Situation

Mr. and Mrs. Thompson had a complex financial situation due to previous financial challenges and irregular income sources. They were concerned about their credit history and the impact it might have on their ability to secure financing for their new home. They sought the assistance of a mortgage broker known for working with borrowers with unique financial circumstances. The mortgage broker analyzed their financial situation, identified areas for improvement, and developed a strategy to address their credit issues. Through the broker's guidance, Mr. and Mrs. Thompson took the necessary steps to improve their credit score and financial stability. The mortgage broker presented their strengthened financial profile to lenders and successfully secured a loan with reasonable terms, allowing them to purchase their desired home.

These real-life case studies demonstrate the value and benefits of working with mortgage brokers. In each scenario, borrowers were able to overcome challenges and secure financing that aligned with their specific needs, thanks to the expertise and guidance of their mortgage brokers. These case studies highlight the importance of partnering with a knowledgeable and experienced mortgage broker who can provide personalized guidance and access to a wide range of loan options. By working with a mortgage broker, borrowers can increase their chances of obtaining favorable financing terms and successfully achieving their real estate goals.

Conclusion

In conclusion, this chapter has highlighted the benefits of working with a mortgage broker in the real estate financing process. Mortgage brokers provide access to a variety of loan options, personalized guidance, and potentially better terms and rates. Case studies have demonstrated how mortgage brokers help borrowers overcome financing challenges and find tailored solutions. By choosing a reputable broker, communicating effectively, and leveraging their expertise, readers can streamline the financing process and increase their chances of achieving their real estate goals.

Chapter 7: Government-Backed Loans

Government - Photo by Katie Moum

7.1 Understanding FHA Loans: Making Homeownership Accessible

FHA loans, offered by the Federal Housing Administration, play a vital role in making homeownership more attainable for low-to-moderate-income borrowers. This section delves into the specifics of FHA loans, providing readers with a comprehensive understanding of their purpose, features, benefits, and eligibility requirements. By exploring the ins and outs of FHA loans, potential homebuyers can make informed decisions about their financing options.

Key Features of FHA Loans

1. *Lower Down Payment Requirements:* One of the key advantages of FHA loans is their lower down payment requirements. While traditional loans often require a

substantial down payment, FHA loans typically require a down payment as low as 3.5% of the purchase price. This lower barrier to entry enables more borrowers to realize their dream of homeownership, even if they have limited savings.

2. *Flexible Credit Criteria:* FHA loans are known for their more lenient credit criteria compared to conventional loans. Borrowers with less-than-perfect credit scores may still be eligible for an FHA loan. The FHA considers factors beyond credit scores, such as payment history and the borrower's ability to repay the loan. This flexibility expands homeownership opportunities for individuals who may have faced challenges in obtaining traditional financing.
3. *Mortgage Insurance*: FHA loans require borrowers to pay mortgage insurance premiums (MIP). This insurance protects the lender in case the borrower defaults on the loan. While the upfront MIP and ongoing monthly premiums increase the cost of the loan, they enable borrowers with lower credit scores or smaller down payments to access favorable loan terms. It's important for borrowers to understand the implications of MIP and factor it into their budgeting.

Benefits of FHA Loans

1. *Accessible Loan Options:* FHA loans cater to borrowers who may not meet the stringent requirements of conventional loans. The program is designed to promote homeownership among individuals with limited financial resources, enabling them to enter the housing market with favorable loan terms.
2. *Lower Interest Rates:* FHA loans often come with competitive interest rates, making them an attractive option for eligible borrowers. These lower rates can result in

significant long-term savings and make homeownership more affordable over the life of the loan.

3. *Streamlined Refinancing:* Another benefit of FHA loans is the option for streamlined refinancing. Borrowers with existing FHA loans can refinance into a new FHA loan without undergoing a full appraisal or extensive documentation process. This streamlined refinancing program simplifies the refinancing process, potentially lowering interest rates or reducing monthly mortgage payments.

Eligibility Requirements for FHA Loans

1. *Minimum Credit Score:* While FHA loans have more flexible credit criteria, borrowers are typically required to have a minimum credit score of 580 to qualify for the 3.5% down payment option. Those with credit scores below 580 may still be eligible but will need to provide a larger down payment, usually 10% of the purchase price.
2. *Debt-to-Income Ratio:* FHA loans have specific guidelines regarding the borrower's debt-to-income ratio (DTI). Generally, the total mortgage payment, including principal, interest, taxes, insurance, and MIP, should not exceed a certain percentage of the borrower's gross monthly income. The specific DTI limits may vary depending on the lender and other factors.
3. *Steady Income and Employment History:* To qualify for an FHA loan, borrowers need to demonstrate a stable employment history and consistent income. Lenders typically require two years of employment and income verification, which can include pay stubs, tax returns, and bank statements.

4. *Property Eligibility:* FHA loans are intended for owner-occupied properties. The property being financed must meet certain criteria, including meeting minimum property standards set by the FHA. It's important for borrowers to ensure the property they wish to purchase meets these requirements to qualify for an FHA loan.

In summary, FHA loans provide an accessible pathway to homeownership for low-to-moderate-income borrowers. They offer lower down payment requirements, flexible credit criteria, and competitive interest rates, making them popular among first-time homebuyers and those with limited financial resources. However, borrowers should consider the costs of mortgage insurance premiums and work on improving their credit scores for more favorable terms.

7.2 VA Loans: Making Homeownership Accessible for Veterans

VA loans, offered by the Department of Veterans Affairs (VA), are designed to assist active-duty military members, veterans, and eligible surviving spouses in achieving homeownership. This section provides an in-depth look at the key features, eligibility requirements, and benefits associated with VA loans. Readers will gain a comprehensive understanding of how VA loans can make homeownership more accessible for those who have served our country.

Eligibility for VA Loans

To be eligible for a VA loan, borrowers must meet certain criteria. This includes serving on active duty for a minimum period during wartime or peacetime, as well as honorable discharge for veterans. Surviving spouses of veterans who died as a result of a service-related disability or while in service may also be eligible. The VA provides a Certificate of Eligibility (COE) to confirm an individual's eligibility for a VA loan.

Advantages of VA Loans

1. *Zero Down Payment Requirements:* One of the most significant advantages of VA loans is the absence of a down payment requirement. Unlike conventional loans that typically require a substantial down payment, VA loans allow eligible borrowers to purchase a home without having to make a down payment. This feature greatly reduces the upfront costs associated with homeownership, making it more accessible for veterans and military members.
2. *Competitive Interest Rates:* VA loans often offer competitive interest rates, which can result in significant long-term savings for borrowers. The VA's guarantee on the loan reduces the lender's risk, allowing them to offer favorable interest rates to borrowers. Lower interest rates mean lower monthly mortgage payments and the potential to save thousands of dollars over the life of the loan.
3. *Limited Closing Costs:* VA loans also come with limited closing costs. The VA places restrictions on the types and amount of closing costs that veterans can be charged, which helps to keep these costs more affordable. In addition, certain fees, such as appraisal fees and credit report fees, may be paid by the seller or lender, further reducing the financial burden on borrowers.

In summary, VA loans are a valuable resource for active-duty military members, veterans, and eligible surviving spouses seeking to achieve homeownership. The zero down payment requirement, competitive interest rates, and limited closing costs make VA loans an attractive financing option. Eligible borrowers should explore the benefits and eligibility criteria of VA loans and work with knowledgeable lenders experienced in VA loan programs to navigate the application process successfully.

7.3 USDA Loans: Promoting Rural Development and Homeownership

USDA loans, offered by the United States Department of Agriculture (USDA), are designed to support rural development and increase homeownership opportunities in eligible areas. This section provides an in-depth exploration of the features, benefits, and eligibility criteria of USDA loans. Readers will gain a comprehensive understanding of how USDA loans can make homeownership more attainable for individuals and families in rural communities.

Features and Benefits of USDA Loans

1. *100% Financing:* One of the primary advantages of USDA loans is the availability of 100% financing. This means that borrowers can finance the entire purchase price of a home without the need for a down payment. This feature makes USDA loans an attractive option for borrowers who may not have significant savings for a down payment, allowing them to achieve homeownership with minimal upfront costs.
2. *Low Interest Rates:* USDA loans offer competitive interest rates, often lower than those of conventional loans. These favorable rates help to reduce monthly mortgage payments, making homeownership more affordable for borrowers. Lower interest rates can also result in long-term savings over the life of the loan, allowing borrowers to build equity in their homes more quickly.
3. *Lenient Credit Requirements:* USDA loans are known for

their more lenient credit requirements compared to traditional loans. While a minimum credit score is still required, USDA loans may be accessible to borrowers with lower credit scores or limited credit history. This provides an opportunity for individuals and families who may have encountered difficulties in obtaining conventional financing to secure a mortgage and become homeowners.

Geographical and Income Eligibility for USDA Loans

USDA loans are specifically targeted at properties located in eligible rural areas. The USDA defines these areas based on population size and proximity to urban centers. Borrowers can use the USDA's online mapping tool to determine whether a specific property is located in an eligible area. In addition to geographical eligibility, there are income limits associated with USDA loans. These limits vary based on the location of the property and the size of the borrower's household. Borrowers must meet the income requirements to be eligible for a USDA loan.

In summary, USDA loans play a crucial role in promoting rural development and increasing homeownership opportunities in eligible areas. The availability of 100% financing, low interest rates, and lenient credit requirements make USDA loans an attractive option for individuals and families in rural communities. Prospective borrowers should familiarize themselves with the geographical and income eligibility criteria for USDA loans and work with knowledgeable lenders experienced in USDA loan programs. By taking advantage of the benefits provided by USDA loans, borrowers can achieve their dreams of homeownership and contribute to the growth and development of rural communities.

7.4 Eligibility Requirements for FHA, VA, and USDA

Loans

Understanding the eligibility requirements for government-backed loan programs is essential for borrowers seeking financing options. This section delves into the specific criteria and qualifications for FHA, VA, and USDA loans. By examining credit score guidelines, income limits, property requirements, and necessary documentation, readers will gain a comprehensive understanding of the eligibility requirements for each loan program.

Eligibility Requirements for FHA Loans

1. *Credit Score Guidelines:* FHA loans are known for their more lenient credit requirements. While there is no specific minimum credit score, borrowers generally need a credit score of at least 580 to qualify for the minimum down payment requirement of 3.5%. However, borrowers with credit scores between 500 and 579 may still be eligible with a higher down payment of 10%.
2. *Income Limits:* FHA loans do not have strict income limits. However, borrowers must have a steady and verifiable source of income to demonstrate their ability to repay the loan. Lenders typically evaluate the borrower's debt-to-income ratio, which should not exceed a certain threshold to ensure affordability.
3. *Property Requirements:* FHA loans have specific property requirements to ensure the property meets certain standards of livability and safety. The property must be the borrower's primary residence, and it must meet minimum property standards set by the FHA, including structural integrity and safety features.

Eligibility Requirements for VA Loans

1. *Service Eligibility:* VA loans are available to active-duty military members, veterans, and eligible surviving spouses. Borrowers must meet specific service requirements, which may include a minimum length of service or discharge status.
2. *Credit Score Guidelines:* The VA does not set a minimum credit score requirement. However, lenders may have their own credit score standards. Generally, a credit score of 620 or higher is preferred to secure favorable loan terms.
3. *Income and Debt-to-Income Ratio:* VA loans do not have strict income limits, but borrowers must have a stable income and meet certain residual income requirements. Lenders also consider the borrower's debt-to-income ratio, which typically should not exceed a certain threshold.

Eligibility Requirements for USDA Loans

1. *Geographical Eligibility:* USDA loans are specifically targeted at properties located in eligible rural areas. Borrowers must ensure that the property they intend to finance is within a designated USDA-eligible area. The USDA provides an online mapping tool to check the eligibility of a specific property.
2. *Income Limits:* USDA loans have income limits based on the location of the property and the size of the borrower's household. Borrowers must meet these income limits to be eligible for a USDA loan. The USDA calculates income based on the borrower's gross income, which includes income from all adult members of the household.
3. *Property Requirements:* USDA loans have property requirements to ensure that the property being financed

meets certain standards. These requirements include the property's location in an eligible rural area, its size and condition, and adequate utilities and services.

In summary, understanding the eligibility requirements for FHA, VA, and USDA loans is crucial for borrowers considering government-backed loan programs. By examining credit score guidelines, income limits, property requirements, and necessary documentation, borrowers can determine their eligibility and take the necessary steps to secure financing. It is important to consult with knowledgeable lenders or mortgage professionals who can guide borrowers through the qualification process and help them navigate the specific requirements for each loan program.

Conclusion

In conclusion, government-backed loans, such as FHA, VA, and USDA loans, offer valuable financing options for borrowers in the real estate market. These programs provide accessible pathways to homeownership with lower down payment requirements and more lenient credit standards. However, borrowers should carefully consider the additional costs and location restrictions associated with these loans. Consulting with experienced professionals is advised to make informed decisions based on individual needs and circumstances.

Chapter 8: Using Retirement Accounts for Real Estate Investing

8.1 Overview of Self-Directed Retirement Accounts

Self-directed retirement accounts have gained popularity as a way for individuals to have more control and flexibility over their retirement funds. Traditional retirement accounts often limit investment options to stocks, bonds, and mutual funds. However, self-directed retirement accounts, such as self-directed IRAs and solo 401(k)s, allow investors to explore a broader range of assets, including real estate, precious metals, private equity, and more. This section provides an overview of self-directed retirement accounts, explaining their concept, benefits, and the investment opportunities they offer.

Understanding Self-Directed IRAs

A self-directed IRA is an individual retirement account that allows investors to have control over their investment decisions. Unlike traditional IRAs, which are managed by financial institutions and offer a limited range of investment options, self-directed IRAs allow investors to *choose from a much broader spectrum of assets*. This includes *real estate properties, private loans, tax liens, private equity*, and more. With a self directed IRA, investors have the freedom to leverage their knowledge and expertise in specific industries or asset classes to potentially generate higher returns.

Benefits of Self-Directed IRAs

One of the key benefits of self-directed IRAs is the flexibility they offer in *diversifying retirement portfolios*. By including alternative assets such as real estate, investors can reduce their exposure to traditional market fluctuations and potentially achieve higher returns. Real estate, in particular, has been a popular choice among self-directed IRA investors due to its potential for long-term appreciation and income generation. Additionally, self-directed IRAs provide investors with *greater control* and the ability to take advantage of investment opportunities that may not be available through traditional retirement accounts.

Understanding Solo 401(k)s

Solo 401(k) plans, also known as individual 401(k)s or self-employed 401(k)s, are retirement plans designed for self-employed individuals or small business owners with *no full-time employees*, other than a spouse. Similar to self-directed IRAs, solo 401(k)s offer a broader range of investment options beyond traditional stocks and bonds. This includes *real estate investments, private placements, loans*, and more. Solo 401(k)s provide individuals with the ability to invest their retirement funds in assets they are familiar with and have expertise in, potentially leading to higher returns.

Benefits of Solo 401(k)s

One of the main advantages of solo 401(k) plans is the ability to make *higher contribution limits* compared to other retirement accounts. As both the employer and employee, self-employed individuals can contribute as an employee (elective deferrals) and as an employer (profit-sharing contributions), allowing for potentially larger contributions and tax advantages. Additionally, solo 401(k)s provide the option for individuals to take out loans from their plan, providing access to capital for personal or business purposes. The flexibility and control offered by solo 401(k)s make them an attractive option for self-employed individuals looking to maximize their retirement savings while having the ability to invest in alternative assets.

In summary, self-directed retirement accounts, such as self-directed IRAs and solo 401(k)s, provide individuals with the opportunity to have more control over their retirement funds and invest in a wider range of assets, including real estate. These accounts offer flexibility and options beyond what is typically available in traditional retirement plans. Self-directed IRAs allow investors to diversify their portfolios with alternative assets, while solo 401(k)s provide self-employed individuals with higher contribution limits and greater investment control.

8.2 Investing in Real Estate with a Self-Directed IRA

Investing in real estate using a self-directed IRA can provide individuals with an opportunity to grow their retirement funds through the appreciation and income generated by real estate assets. This section explores the guidelines and procedures for investing in real estate using a self-directed IRA. Readers will gain a deeper understanding of the steps involved in setting up a self-directed IRA, identifying eligible real estate investment opportunities, conducting due diligence, and managing the property within the IRA structure.

Setting up a Self-Directed IRA

The first step in investing in real estate with a self-directed IRA is to establish a *self-directed IRA custodial account* with a qualified custodian that specializes in handling alternative assets. The custodian will handle the administrative tasks and ensure compliance with IRS regulations. It is important to choose a custodian experienced in handling self-directed IRAs to ensure a smooth process. Once the account is set up, funds from an existing IRA or rollover funds can be transferred to the self-directed IRA custodial account.

Identifying Eligible Real Estate Investment Opportunities

With a self-directed IRA, investors have the flexibility to invest in various types of real estate properties, including *residential*, *commercial*, *multifamily*, and even *raw land*. However, there are certain restrictions to be aware of. The IRS prohibits self-directed IRA owners from investing in properties they *currently own* or using IRA funds to purchase properties for *personal use*. Additionally, any income generated by the property must flow back into the IRA. It is important to work with a knowledgeable real estate agent or investment advisor who understands the rules and regulations surrounding self-directed IRAs to identify eligible investment opportunities.

Conducting Due Diligence

Just like any other real estate investment, conducting thorough due diligence is crucial when investing with a self-directed IRA. This includes researching the property's *market value*, potential *rental income*, *location*, and any associated expenses such as property taxes, insurance, and maintenance costs. It is also essential to review the seller's terms and conditions, assess the property's condition through inspections, and verify the property's title and legal documentation. Due diligence is key to ensuring that the investment aligns with the investor's financial goals and risk tolerance.

Managing the Property within the IRA Structure

Once the real estate investment is made, it is important to understand that all income and expenses related to the property must *flow through the self-directed IRA*. Rental income, property taxes, maintenance costs, and other expenses must be paid using funds from the IRA account. Additionally, any capital improvements or repairs made to the property must also be funded by the IRA. It is crucial to maintain accurate records and documentation of all transactions to *ensure compliance with IRS regulations*. Working with a property manager or a professional real estate management company can help streamline the process and ensure the property is managed within the IRA structure.

Investing in real estate with a self-directed IRA can provide individuals with a unique opportunity to grow their retirement funds through real estate assets. By understanding the guidelines and procedures involved in setting up a self-directed IRA, identifying eligible investment opportunities, conducting due diligence, and managing the property within the IRA structure, investors can navigate the complexities of real estate investing within the framework of a self-directed IRA. It is important to work with experienced professionals who specialize in self-directed IRAs and real estate investments to ensure compliance with IRS regulations and maximize the potential benefits of this investment strategy.

8.3 Tax Benefits of Using Retirement Accounts for Real

Estate Investing

Utilizing retirement accounts for real estate investing can offer significant tax benefits and advantages. This section explores the tax benefits associated with using retirement accounts, such as self-directed IRAs and solo 401(k)s, for real estate investments. Readers will gain an understanding of the potential tax advantages, including tax-deferred or tax-free growth, deductions for real estate expenses, and the potential for tax-free distributions upon retirement.

Tax-Deferred or Tax-Free Growth

One of the primary tax benefits of using retirement accounts for real estate investing is the potential for *tax-deferred* or *tax-free growth of investments*. Within a self-directed IRA or solo 401(k), any income or gains generated from real estate investments are typically *sheltered from immediate taxation*. This allows the investments to grow and compound over time without the burden of annual tax payments. As a result, individuals have the opportunity to accumulate more wealth and increase their retirement savings.

Deductions for Real Estate Expenses

Real estate investing often involves various expenses, such as property management fees, repairs and maintenance costs, and property taxes. When using retirement accounts for real estate investments, individuals may be eligible to deduct these expenses, which can help reduce their overall tax liability. Deductible expenses can offset the income generated from rental properties or real estate businesses, resulting in lower taxable income and potentially higher after-tax returns.

Tax-Free Distributions in Retirement

Another significant tax benefit of using retirement accounts for real estate investing is the potential for tax-free distributions in retirement. Traditional IRAs and 401(k) accounts are subject to taxation upon withdrawal. However, utilizing a Roth self-directed IRA or a Roth solo 401(k) allows individuals to contribute after-tax dollars into the account and potentially enjoy *tax-free distributions in retirement.* This means that any income or gains from real estate investments within a Roth account can be withdrawn tax-free, providing individuals with a tax-efficient source of income during retirement.

Considerations and Limitations

While the tax benefits of using retirement accounts for real estate investing are substantial, it is important to consider certain limitations and factors. For example, prohibited transactions and self-dealing rules must be strictly followed to maintain the tax advantages associated with retirement accounts. Engaging the services of a qualified tax professional or financial advisor who specializes in self-directed retirement accounts can help ensure compliance with IRS regulations and optimize the tax benefits.

Additionally, it is crucial to note that while real estate expenses may be deductible, the ability to claim these deductions depends on various factors, including the type of retirement account, the specific expenses, and the individual's tax situation. Consulting with a tax professional can provide personalized guidance regarding eligible deductions and maximize the tax benefits.

In summary, utilizing retirement accounts, such as self-directed IRAs and solo 401(k)s, for real estate investing can offer significant tax benefits. The potential for tax-deferred or tax-free growth, deductions for real estate expenses, and the possibility of tax-free distributions in retirement make these accounts attractive options for real estate investors. However, it is crucial to understand the rules and regulations surrounding retirement account investments and consult with tax professionals to ensure compliance and optimize tax benefits.

8.4 Risks and Considerations of Using Retirement Accounts for Real Estate Investing

While using retirement accounts for real estate investing can offer numerous advantages, it is essential to consider the associated risks and considerations. This section explores the potential challenges and factors individuals should be aware of when utilizing retirement accounts, such as self-directed IRAs and solo 401(k)s, for real estate investments. Readers will gain a comprehensive understanding of the risks involved and the considerations they need to take into account.

Liquidity Constraints

One of the significant risks of using retirement accounts for real estate investing is the potential liquidity constraints. Unlike traditional investments such as stocks or bonds, real estate investments typically require a significant amount of capital and may lack the same level of liquidity. Once funds are invested in real estate within a retirement account, they are *tied up and may not be readily available* for other financial needs or emergencies. Individuals must carefully consider their cash flow requirements and ensure they have sufficient funds outside of their retirement accounts for unexpected expenses.

Administrative Responsibilities

Investing in real estate through retirement accounts involves additional administrative responsibilities. Individuals are responsible for *ensuring compliance with IRS regulations*, maintaining accurate records, and submitting the necessary paperwork for transactions within the account. Failure to meet these administrative requirements may result in penalties or the *loss of tax advantages* associated with retirement accounts. It is crucial to understand the administrative responsibilities involved and be prepared to fulfill them or seek professional assistance to navigate the complexities.

Penalties for Non-Compliance

Non-compliance with IRS regulations and rules regarding retirement account investments can have *severe consequences*. Engaging in prohibited transactions or engaging in self-dealing, such as using retirement funds to purchase property for personal use, can result in *substantial penalties* and *tax liabilities*. It is essential to understand and adhere to IRS guidelines to maintain the tax advantages of retirement accounts and avoid costly penalties.

Due Diligence

Proper due diligence is critical when using retirement accounts for real estate investing. Individuals must carefully evaluate potential investment opportunities, assess the risks, and conduct thorough research on the properties or real estate ventures before making a decision. This includes *assessing the market conditions*, *evaluating the property's potential for appreciation or rental income*, and considering any potential *legal or regulatory issues*. Thorough due diligence helps mitigate risks and ensures that investments align with the individual's investment goals and risk tolerance.

In summary, using retirement accounts for real estate investing offers unique opportunities but also comes with risks and considerations. Understanding the liquidity constraints, administrative responsibilities, potential penalties for non-compliance, and the need for proper due diligence is crucial for individuals looking to utilize their retirement accounts for real estate investments. By carefully evaluating the risks, seeking professional guidance when necessary, and conducting thorough due diligence, individuals can make informed decisions and navigate the complexities of real estate investing within retirement accounts.

Conclusion

Utilizing retirement accounts for real estate investing offers individuals the opportunity to diversify their portfolios and enjoy potential tax advantages. However, careful consideration, thorough research, and compliance with IRS regulations are crucial. Investors should seek professional advice, evaluate liquidity constraints, administrative responsibilities, and penalties, and conduct due diligence. Maintaining compliance is essential to preserve tax advantages. By making informed decisions and adhering to guidelines, investors can maximize the benefits of real estate investing within retirement accounts and enhance their long-term savings.

Chapter 9: Hard Money and Private Money Loans

9.1 What are Hard Money and Private Money Loans?

In the world of real estate investing, traditional financing options are not always readily available or suitable for every situation. That's where hard money and private money loans come into play. These alternative financing options provide borrowers with the flexibility and accessibility they need to fund their real estate projects. This section will provide an overview of hard money and private money loans, explaining their differences and how they are commonly used in the realm of real estate investing.

Understanding Hard Money Loans

Hard money loans are short-term loans that are typically secured by real estate collateral. Unlike traditional loans, hard money loans are issued by private investors or companies, known as hard money lenders, rather than banks or financial institutions. These loans are often sought by real estate investors who require *quick access to funds* or have *difficulty obtaining financing through traditional channels* due to factors such as credit issues or the condition of the property.

Key Features of Hard Money Loans

Hard money loans have distinct features that differentiate them from traditional loans.

1. Firstly, they are typically *short-term loans* with a duration ranging from a few months to a few years. This shorter term allows borrowers to quickly acquire and renovate properties before either selling them or refinancing with a conventional loan.
2. Secondly, hard money loans are *asset-based*, meaning that the value of the property being used as collateral plays a significant role in the loan approval process. This allows borrowers with less-than-perfect credit or unconventional investment strategies to access financing.

Exploring Private Money Loans

Private money loans, on the other hand, are loans that are provided by private individuals or companies, often referred to as private money lenders. These lenders can include *family members*, *friends*, or other individuals who have capital available for investment purposes. Private money loans are typically negotiated between the borrower and the lender, allowing for greater flexibility in terms and conditions compared to traditional loans. They can be used for various purposes, including real estate acquisitions, renovations, or even starting a business.

Benefits and Considerations of Hard Money and Private Money Loans

Both hard money and private money loans offer unique benefits and considerations for borrowers.

1. The primary advantage is the ability to *obtain financing quickly*, bypassing the lengthy approval process of traditional lenders. This speed can be crucial in competitive real estate markets where time is of the essence.
2. Additionally, hard money and private money lenders are often *more lenient* when it comes to credit requirements, making these loan options accessible to borrowers with less-than-perfect credit histories.
3. However, it is important to note that hard money and private money loans often come with *higher interest rates* and fees compared to traditional loans. This is due to the increased risk assumed by the lenders, as they are primarily focused on the value of the property being used as collateral.

Borrowers must carefully consider the **cost of borrowing** and ensure that the potential profits from their real estate investments outweigh the expenses associated with these loans.

Hard money and private money loans provide real estate investors with alternative financing options that can be instrumental in funding their projects. Understanding the differences between hard money and private money loans, as well as their benefits and considerations, is essential for investors looking to explore these financing options. By leveraging the speed and flexibility offered by these loans, investors can seize time-sensitive opportunities, overcome credit challenges, and maximize their real estate investment potential.

9.2 How to Find Hard Money and Private Money Lenders

Once you've decided to explore hard money and private money loans as financing options for your real estate investments, the next step is finding the right lenders. While traditional lenders are easily accessible through banks and financial institutions, the search for hard money and private money lenders requires a different approach. This section will explore various strategies and resources you can utilize to find hard money and private money lenders for your real estate projects.

Networking and Building Relationships

One of the most effective ways to find hard money and private money lenders is through networking and building relationships within the real estate industry. Attend local *real estate investment meetings*, join *real estate investment associations*, and actively participate in *online forums and communities*. Engaging with other investors, real estate professionals, and lenders themselves can provide valuable connections and potential leads on private lenders who may be willing to fund your projects.

Real Estate Investment Events

Attending real estate investment events, conferences, and seminars can be an excellent way to connect with hard money and private money lenders. These events often attract industry professionals, including lenders who specialize in real estate financing. Take the opportunity to network, exchange business cards, and have conversations with lenders during these events. You may find lenders who are actively seeking investment opportunities and are open to financing your real estate projects.

Online Platforms and Directories

The internet has made it easier than ever to connect with potential lenders. *Online platforms* and *directories* dedicated to private lending can be valuable resources in your search for hard money and private money lenders. Websites such as *BiggerPockets*, *PrivateLenderLink*, and *Connected Investors* provide platforms where lenders and borrowers can connect. These platforms typically allow you to create a profile, list your funding needs, and connect with lenders who align with your financing requirements.

Referrals from Industry Professionals

Industry professionals, such as real estate agents, mortgage brokers, and real estate attorneys, often have connections with hard money and private money lenders. They work closely with investors and lenders on a regular basis and can provide *valuable referrals*. Reach out to professionals in your network and let them know you are looking for private financing. They may be able to recommend lenders they have worked with in the past or have knowledge of lenders who are actively funding real estate projects.

Due Diligence and Selection Process

Finding potential lenders is just the beginning. It's crucial to conduct thorough due diligence on each lender you come across to ensure they are *reputable and suitable for your financing needs*. Consider factors such as their experience in real estate lending, their track record, the terms and conditions they offer, and the level of transparency in their operations. Request references and speak with other borrowers who have worked with the lender to get a better understanding of their reliability and responsiveness.

Finding hard money and private money lenders requires a proactive approach and leveraging various resources available to real estate investors. Networking, attending investment events, utilizing online platforms, and seeking referrals from industry professionals can help you connect with potential lenders. However, it's essential to conduct thorough due diligence on each lender to ensure they are reputable and align with your financing requirements.

9.3 Qualifying for Hard Money and Private Money Loans

Qualifying for hard money and private money loans is different from traditional loan programs offered by banks and financial institutions. These alternative financing options focus more on the collateral value of the property and the borrower's real estate investment experience rather than creditworthiness. In this section, we will explore the qualifications and criteria that lenders typically consider when evaluating loan applications for hard money and private money loans.

Collateral and Property Value

One of the primary factors that hard money and private money lenders assess is the collateral value of the property being financed. Since these loans are *asset-based*, lenders prioritize the value and potential for the property to generate returns. They may conduct a thorough *appraisal and assessment* to determine the property's *market value*, *condition*, *location*, and *income potential*. A higher property value and equity can increase the chances of loan approval and may even allow for more favorable loan terms.

Creditworthiness and Experience

While creditworthiness is less of a concern for hard money and private money lenders compared to traditional lenders, *some level of credit evaluation* may still be conducted. Lenders may review credit scores and histories to assess the borrower's general financial responsibility and potential risks. However, even borrowers with lower credit scores or past credit issues may still be eligible for these loans if the property value and investment opportunity are strong.

In addition to creditworthiness, lenders also consider the *borrower's experience* in real estate investing. They may prefer borrowers who have a track record of successful real estate projects or relevant industry experience. This is because they want to ensure that the borrower has the knowledge and skills to manage the property and maximize its value.

Down Payment and Equity

Hard money and private money loans typically require a *significant down payment* or equity in the property. Lenders often expect borrowers to have a stake in the investment to minimize their own risk. The specific down payment or equity requirements can *vary depending on the lender* and the property type. In some cases, lenders may provide financing based on a percentage of the property's after-repair value (ARV), taking into account the potential increase in value after renovations or improvements.

Exit Strategy

Another crucial aspect lenders consider is the borrower's exit strategy. They want assurance that the borrower has a *clear plan to repay the loan*, either through the sale of the property, refinancing with a traditional lender, or using other funds. Lenders may evaluate the feasibility of the exit strategy and the potential risks associated with it. Having a well-thought-out exit strategy that aligns with the loan term and repayment expectations can significantly increase the likelihood of loan approval.

Qualifying for hard money and private money loans requires a focus on different factors compared to traditional loans. While creditworthiness is considered, lenders primarily prioritize the collateral value of the property, the borrower's experience in real estate investing, and the down payment or equity. Having a solid exit strategy is also crucial. Understanding the qualifications and criteria that lenders look for can help borrowers prepare their loan applications and increase their chances of obtaining financing for their real estate projects. It's important to work closely with lenders, be transparent about your financial and investment circumstances, and demonstrate your commitment to the project's success.

9.4 The Benefits and Drawbacks of Hard Money and Private Money Loans

Hard money and private money loans have gained popularity as alternative financing options in the real estate industry. These loan options provide borrowers with access to funds from private individuals or companies, bypassing traditional financial institutions. While they offer unique advantages, it is important for borrowers to consider the potential drawbacks. This section examines the benefits and drawbacks of hard money and private money loans, providing readers with a balanced understanding of these loan options.

Benefits of Hard Money and Private Money Loans

1. *Faster Approval and Funding:* One of the major advantages of hard money and private money loans is the speed of approval and funding. Unlike traditional loans that involve lengthy application processes and underwriting procedures, hard

money and private money loans can be approved and funded within a matter of days or weeks. This quick turnaround time is beneficial for real estate investors who need immediate financing to seize time-sensitive opportunities.

2. *Flexibility in Loan Terms:* Hard money and private money lenders are often more flexible in their loan terms compared to traditional lenders. They have the ability to tailor loan terms to meet the specific needs of the borrower and the property being financed. This flexibility can include options for interest-only payments, shorter loan durations, and customized repayment schedules. Such flexibility allows borrowers to structure the loan in a way that aligns with their investment strategy and financial goals.
3. *Access to Financing for Non-Traditional Properties or Borrowers:* Hard money and private money loans provide financing options for properties that may not meet the strict criteria of traditional lenders. They are often more willing to finance non-traditional properties such as fix-and-flip projects, distressed properties, or properties in need of significant renovations. Additionally, these loans can be accessible to borrowers with less-than-perfect credit histories, as lenders primarily focus on the value of the property being used as collateral.

Drawbacks of Hard Money and Private Money Loans

1. *Higher Interest Rates and Fees:* One of the main drawbacks of hard money and private money loans is the higher cost compared to traditional loans. Interest rates for these loans tend to be higher, reflecting the increased risk undertaken by the lenders. Additionally, borrowers may also encounter higher fees, such as origination fees and prepayment

penalties. It is crucial for borrowers to carefully evaluate the overall cost of the loan and consider whether the benefits outweigh the higher expenses.

2. *Shorter Loan Terms:* Hard money and private money loans often come with shorter loan terms compared to traditional loans. While this can be advantageous for borrowers who plan to quickly renovate and sell a property or refinance with a conventional loan, it can also pose challenges for those who require longer-term financing. Borrowers need to ensure they have a viable exit strategy to repay the loan within the designated time frame.
3. *Limited Consumer Protection:* Another drawback of hard money and private money loans is the limited consumer protection compared to traditional loans. These loans are typically not subject to the same regulations and oversight as traditional loans, which can expose borrowers to potentially unfavorable terms or practices. It is crucial for borrowers to conduct thorough due diligence, research lenders carefully, and seek legal advice if needed to protect their interests.

Hard money and private money loans offer unique advantages for real estate investors who need quick access to financing or have properties that may not meet traditional lending criteria. The speed of approval, flexibility in loan terms, and accessibility for borrowers with less-than-perfect credit make these loan options appealing. However, borrowers must also consider the potential drawbacks, including higher interest rates and fees, shorter loan terms, and limited consumer protection. By carefully weighing the pros and cons, borrowers can make informed decisions regarding the use of hard money and private money loans in their real estate ventures.

9.5 How to Negotiate Loan Terms and Rates with Hard Money and Private Money Lenders

Negotiating loan terms and rates with hard money and private money lenders can significantly impact the overall cost and feasibility of real estate investments. This section aims to provide readers with guidance on effectively negotiating loan terms and rates with these alternative lenders. By understanding the factors that influence negotiations and implementing effective strategies, borrowers can potentially secure more favorable loan terms that align with their investment goals.

Factors Influencing Negotiations

1. *Loan Amount:* The loan amount plays a crucial role in negotiations. Higher loan amounts may provide borrowers with more leverage to negotiate better terms and rates. Lenders are more likely to be flexible when the loan amount represents a significant portion of the property's value or when the borrower has a strong track record of successful investments.
2. *Interest Rates:* Interest rates are a key consideration in loan negotiations. Borrowers should research prevailing market rates for similar types of loans and use that information as a basis for negotiation. Demonstrating knowledge of current market rates and competitive offers from other lenders can empower borrowers to negotiate for more favorable interest rates.
3. *Loan-to-Value (LTV) Ratio:* The loan-to-value ratio represents the percentage of the property's value that the lender is willing to finance. Negotiating a lower LTV ratio can reduce the borrower's risk and potentially lead to more favorable loan terms. Borrowers should present compelling reasons why a lower LTV ratio is justified, such as a solid

investment strategy, favorable property characteristics, or a strong borrower profile.

4. *Repayment Terms:* Negotiating repayment terms, such as loan duration and payment schedule, is essential for borrowers to align the loan with their investment strategy and financial capabilities. Longer loan durations can provide more flexibility, while shorter durations may lead to better terms. Borrowers should evaluate their investment timeline and financial projections to determine the most favorable repayment terms and negotiate accordingly.

Effective Negotiation Strategies

1. *Research and Preparation:* Thoroughly research the lender's background, lending criteria, and typical loan terms before entering into negotiations. Understanding the lender's preferences and limitations will enable borrowers to present well-informed proposals and negotiate from a position of knowledge and confidence.
2. *Demonstrate Credibility and Track Record:* Highlighting a strong track record of successful real estate investments and financial stability can significantly enhance negotiating power. Provide documentation of past projects, financial statements, and references to demonstrate credibility and reassure lenders of the borrower's ability to meet loan obligations.
3. *Compare Multiple Offers:* Solicit multiple offers from different hard money and private money lenders to create competition and leverage during negotiations. Presenting competing offers can encourage lenders to offer more competitive terms and rates to secure the borrower's business.
4. *Seek Professional Guidance:* Consider working with an

experienced real estate attorney or consultant who specializes in negotiating with private lenders. Their expertise and knowledge of industry practices can provide valuable insights and help navigate the negotiation process effectively.

5. *Be Flexible and Open to Compromise:* While it is important to negotiate for favorable terms, borrowers should also be open to compromise. Recognize that lenders have their own risk assessment criteria and profit expectations. By finding a balance that benefits both parties, borrowers can increase the chances of reaching a mutually satisfactory agreement.

Negotiating loan terms and rates with hard money and private money lenders requires careful research, preparation, and effective communication. By considering factors such as loan amount, interest rates, loan-to-value ratios, and repayment terms, borrowers can identify areas for negotiation and potentially secure more favorable loan terms. Implementing effective negotiation strategies, such as demonstrating credibility, comparing offers, seeking professional guidance, and being flexible, can enhance the borrower's ability to secure the best possible loan terms and rates for their real estate investment ventures.

9.6 Tips for Successful Hard Money and Private Money Financing

Securing hard money and private money financing can be a valuable tool for real estate investors. To ensure a successful financing experience, it's important to approach the process with careful planning and execution. In this section, we will provide practical tips to help you navigate the world of hard money and private money financing and increase your chances of success.

1. Conduct Thorough Due Diligence

Before entering into any financing agreement, it's essential to conduct thorough due diligence. This includes researching and evaluating potential lenders, reviewing their track record, reputation, and customer feedback. Verify their credentials, licenses, and experience in providing hard money or private money loans. Additionally, conduct a comprehensive analysis of the property you intend to finance, including its market value, potential risks, and income-generating capabilities. Understanding the lender and property will help you make informed decisions and mitigate potential risks.

2. Prepare a Compelling Loan Application

To increase your chances of loan approval, it's crucial to prepare a compelling loan application. Provide accurate and complete information about *yourself*, your *real estate investment experience*, and your *financial situation*. Include a detailed description of the *property*, its *current condition*, and your *plans for renovation* or improvement. Present a solid business plan that outlines the investment strategy, projected returns, and your exit strategy. Remember to highlight the potential value of the property and how it aligns with the lender's criteria. A well-prepared and persuasive loan application can significantly impact the lender's decision.

3. Maintain Open Communication

Establishing and maintaining open communication with the lender is vital throughout the financing process. Respond promptly to their inquiries and requests for additional documentation. Keep them informed about any changes or updates regarding the property or your investment plan. Clear and transparent communication builds trust and shows your commitment to the success of the project. It also allows you to address any concerns or questions the lender may have, ensuring a smoother financing experience.

4. Manage the Loan Effectively

Once you secure the hard money or private money financing, it's important to manage the loan effectively. Stay organized and *keep detailed records* of all loan-related documents, payments, and expenses. Adhere to the terms and conditions outlined in the loan agreement, including interest payments, repayment schedule, and any other obligations. Regularly monitor the progress of the project and communicate any significant developments or challenges to the lender. By effectively managing the loan, you demonstrate your professionalism and commitment to fulfilling your obligations.

5. Build Relationships and Network

Building relationships and networking within the real estate industry can be beneficial for *securing future financing opportunities*. Attend industry events, join real estate investment groups, and connect with other professionals in the field. Networking allows you to meet potential lenders, brokers, and other investors who may provide valuable insights and opportunities. By building a strong network, you increase your chances of finding suitable financing options and expanding your real estate investment portfolio.

Successful hard money and private money financing require careful preparation, thorough due diligence, and effective management. By conducting thorough research, preparing a compelling loan application, maintaining open communication, managing the loan effectively, and building relationships within the industry, you can increase your chances of securing financing for your real estate projects.

Remember, each financing opportunity is unique, so adapt these tips to your specific circumstances and work closely with lenders to ensure a successful financing experience.

Conclusion

In summary, hard money and private money loans offer real estate investors alternative financing options that can provide flexibility and expedited access to funds. By understanding the nature of these loans, conducting thorough due diligence, and effectively managing the financing process, investors can increase their chances of success in securing and utilizing these loan options. Networking, building relationships, and maintaining open communication with lenders are key factors in establishing a successful financing experience. Additionally, borrowers should carefully consider the pros and cons of hard money and private money loans and tailor their strategies to align with their investment goals and risk tolerance. With proper planning and execution, these loan options can be valuable tools for real estate investors seeking to grow their portfolios and achieve their financial objectives.

Chapter 10: Real Estate Investment Partnerships

Parners - Photo by Sebastian Herrmann

10.1 Overview of Real Estate Investment Partnerships:

Real estate investment partnerships have become increasingly popular in the real estate industry as a way for individuals to combine their financial resources and expertise to pursue profitable investment opportunities. This section provides an overview of real estate investment partnerships, explaining the concept, structure, and benefits of forming partnerships for real estate investments. By understanding the basics of real estate investment partnerships, readers will be equipped with valuable knowledge to consider this investment strategy.

The Concept of Real Estate Investment Partnerships

A real estate investment partnership is a *collaborative venture* where *two or more individuals* come together to pool their financial resources, skills, and experience to invest in real estate properties. The partners typically *share the profits, losses*, and responsibilities of the investment in proportion to their contribution or agreement. This partnership structure allows individuals to leverage their combined resources and expertise to access larger and more lucrative real estate deals that may not be feasible as individual investors.

Benefits of Real Estate Investment Partnerships

Real estate investment partnerships offer numerous benefits to individuals looking to invest in real estate. Some of the key advantages include:

1. *Increased Capital and Buying Power:* By pooling financial resources, partners can accumulate a larger amount of capital to fund real estate investments. This increased buying power allows partners to pursue larger and potentially more profitable properties that would be difficult to acquire individually.
2. *Shared Expertise and Responsibilities:* Real estate investment partnerships bring together individuals with diverse skills, knowledge, and experiences. Each partner can contribute their expertise in areas such as property analysis, financing, property management, or legal matters, which enhances the overall decision-making process and operational efficiency of the partnership.
3. *Risk Mitigation:* Investing in real estate inherently carries risks. However, real estate investment partnerships can help

mitigate these risks by spreading them among multiple partners. If one property or investment performs poorly, the partnership's overall portfolio may still remain strong due to the diversity of investments.

4. *Access to Specialized Opportunities:* Partnerships can create opportunities to invest in specialized real estate sectors or strategies that require specific expertise or resources. For example, a partnership might focus on commercial properties, residential rentals, fix-and-flip projects, or development opportunities, leveraging the partners' combined knowledge and resources to maximize returns.
5. *Networking and Industry Connections:* Real estate investment partnerships provide access to a wider network of industry professionals, including brokers, lenders, contractors, and property managers. These connections can open doors to new investment opportunities, provide valuable market insights, and facilitate the overall success of the partnership.

Considerations for Real Estate Investment Partnerships

While real estate investment partnerships offer numerous benefits, it is important to consider certain factors before forming or joining a partnership:

1. *Shared Vision and Goals:* Partners should have aligned investment objectives, risk tolerance, and long-term goals. It is crucial to have open and honest discussions to ensure compatibility and avoid conflicts down the line.
2. *Legal and Financial Structure:* Partnerships should have a clear legal and financial structure, outlining the rights, responsibilities, profit-sharing arrangements, decision-making processes, and exit strategies. Consulting with legal

and financial professionals is recommended to establish a solid foundation for the partnership.

3. *Trust and Communication:* Trust and effective communication among partners are essential for a successful real estate investment partnership. Partners should be able to openly discuss concerns, share information, and make collaborative decisions that benefit the partnership as a whole.
4. *Roles and Responsibilities:* Clearly defining each partner's roles, responsibilities, and areas of expertise helps ensure that everyone contributes effectively and avoids duplication of efforts. This clarity helps streamline operations and maximizes the partnership's overall efficiency.
5. *Exit Strategies and Dissolution:* It is important to establish procedures for exiting the partnership or dissolving it if necessary. These procedures should outline how assets are distributed, debts are settled, and the partnership's reputation is maintained throughout the dissolution process.
6. *Legal and Regulatory Compliance:* Real estate investment partnerships must comply with applicable laws and regulations. Partners should be aware of any licensing requirements, zoning regulations, tax obligations, and other legal considerations that may impact the partnership's operations. Consulting with legal and tax professionals can ensure compliance and mitigate potential risks.
7. *Personal and Financial Compatibility:* Real estate investment partnerships require a certain level of personal and financial compatibility among partners. It is important to assess the financial stability, investment track record, and overall commitment of potential partners before entering into a partnership. Trusting the partners' financial capabilities and dedication to the partnership is crucial for a successful

collaboration.

Real estate investment partnerships offer individuals the opportunity to leverage resources and expertise for collective real estate investments. The benefits include increased buying power, shared expertise, risk mitigation, specialized opportunities, and networking advantages. However, careful consideration of shared goals, legal and financial structures, trust, communication, and defined roles is necessary. Compliance with regulations and personal compatibility is also important.

10.2 Types of Real Estate Investment Partnerships

Before entering into a partnership, it's crucial to understand the different types of real estate investment partnerships available. This section will delve into three common types: general partnerships, limited partnerships, and limited liability partnerships, providing insights into their structures and legal considerations.

1. General Partnerships

A general partnership is a straightforward and common type of real estate investment partnership. In this arrangement, all partners share *equal responsibility and liability* for the partnership's actions and debts. Each partner has *an active role* in the decision-making process, property management, and day-to-day operations. General partnerships are often established through a formal partnership agreement that outlines the partners' responsibilities, profit-sharing arrangements, and procedures for dispute resolution.

One of the significant advantages of a general partnership is the *shared management responsibilities*, allowing partners to contribute their unique skills and expertise. However, it's important to note that all partners have *unlimited personal liability* for the partnership's obligations. This means that if the partnership faces legal issues or financial difficulties, each partner can be held personally responsible. Therefore, it's crucial to choose trustworthy and reliable partners when considering a general partnership.

2. Limited Partnerships

Limited partnerships offer a more flexible structure compared to general partnerships. In this type of partnership, there are two distinct roles: general partners and limited partners.

1. The *general partner* is responsible for managing the partnership's operations, while
2. *limited partners* are passive investors who contribute capital but have limited involvement in decision-making.

The primary advantage of a limited partnership is that *limited partners have limited liability*. Their liability is restricted to the amount of their investment, protecting their personal assets from the partnership's obligations. This arrangement often appeals to investors who wish to participate in real estate ventures without actively managing the properties. Limited partnerships are typically governed by a partnership agreement that outlines the general partner's authority, profit distribution, and mechanisms for admitting new partners.

3. Limited Liability Partnerships

(LLPs) provide *a balance between general partnerships and limited liability companies (LLCs)*. LLPs offer the benefits of limited liability, similar to an LLC, while allowing partners to have direct involvement in the partnership's management and decision-making processes.

In an LLP, each partner's liability is *limited to their investment in the partnership*, shielding their personal assets from the partnership's debts and obligations. This structure provides a level of protection while allowing partners to actively participate in the real estate investment activities. LLPs are often preferred by professionals such as attorneys, accountants, or real estate agents who want to form a partnership while limiting their personal liability.

Legal Considerations

When establishing a real estate investment partnership, it's crucial to consider the legal implications associated with each type of partnership. Partnerships are subject to specific regulations and requirements that vary depending on the jurisdiction. Consulting with a legal professional specializing in real estate law is recommended to ensure compliance with local laws and to draft a comprehensive partnership agreement.

The partnership agreement should outline the partners' roles, responsibilities, profit-sharing arrangements, dispute resolution mechanisms, and provisions for adding or removing partners. It should also address potential scenarios such as the death or withdrawal of a partner and the distribution of assets in the event of dissolution.

In summary, understanding the various types of real estate investment partnerships is essential before entering into any partnership. General partnerships, limited partnerships, and limited liability partnerships each offer distinct structures and legal considerations. General partnerships allow for shared management responsibilities but also come with unlimited personal liability for each partner. Limited partnerships provide flexibility and limited liability for passive investors. Limited liability partnerships strike a balance between general partnerships and limited liability companies, offering limited liability while allowing partners to actively participate in management. When establishing a real estate partnership, consulting with a legal professional is crucial to ensure compliance with local laws and draft a comprehensive partnership agreement that addresses roles, responsibilities, profit-sharing, dispute resolution, and potential scenarios.

10.3 Qualifying for Real Estate Investment Partnerships

Participating in a real estate investment partnership can be an exciting opportunity to leverage resources, knowledge, and capital to pursue profitable ventures in the real estate market. However, not everyone may be eligible to join or form a partnership. This section will explore the qualifications and criteria that potential partners typically consider when establishing or joining a real estate investment partnership.

Financial Resources

Real estate investment partnerships often require a *significant financial commitment from each partner*. Partners should have the financial resources to contribute to the partnership's capital requirements and ongoing expenses. This may include funds for property acquisitions, renovations, maintenance costs, property management fees, and other operational expenses. Partners may be evaluated based on their ability to make substantial financial contributions to the partnership and their financial stability.

Expertise and Experience

Expertise and experience in the real estate industry are highly valued qualifications for potential partners. *Each partner brings their unique skills*, knowledge, and network to the partnership, contributing to its success. Partners with a background in real estate development, property management, finance, legal, or other related fields can add significant value by providing insights, analysis, and guidance in the decision-making process. Prior experience in real estate investments and a track record of successful ventures may also be considered when evaluating potential partners.

Shared Investment Goals and Strategy

Alignment of investment goals and strategies is crucial for a successful real estate investment partnership. Partners should have compatible investment objectives, risk tolerance, and a shared vision for the partnership. It's essential to discuss and agree upon factors such as the desired *investment duration*, *target property types* (residential, commercial, industrial, etc.), *geographic locations*, *expected returns*, and *exit strategies*. Partners should have a clear understanding of each other's investment preferences to ensure a cohesive and productive partnership.

Trust and Compatibility

Building a real estate investment partnership requires trust and compatibility among partners. Trust is essential in a partnership as it involves pooling financial resources and making joint investment decisions. Partners should have a *mutual understanding*, *respect*, and *trust* in each other's abilities, integrity, and commitment to the partnership. Compatibility in terms of work ethic, communication styles, and decision-making processes is also important for a harmonious partnership.

Contribution and Commitment

Partnerships thrive when *all members actively contribute* and remain committed to the partnership's goals. Potential partners should be willing to *actively participate, share responsibilities*, and *contribute their time, skills*, and *resources* to the partnership's activities. This may include property research, due diligence, negotiations, financing arrangements, property management, or other tasks necessary for successful real estate investments. Commitment to the long-term success of the partnership, as well as open and transparent communication, are crucial qualities for potential partners.

In summary, Participating in a real estate investment partnership requires meeting certain qualifications and criteria. Financial resources, expertise and experience in the real estate industry, shared investment goals, trust and compatibility among partners, and a commitment to contribute and remain actively involved are important factors that potential partners consider. By evaluating these qualifications and criteria, real estate investment partnerships can be formed with individuals or groups who bring complementary skills, resources, and perspectives, leading to successful and profitable ventures in the dynamic real estate market.

10.4 Advantages and Disadvantages of Real Estate Investment Partnerships

While these partnerships can provide numerous benefits, it's important to understand the advantages and disadvantages before entering into such an arrangement. This section will explore the pros and cons of real estate investment partnerships to provide readers with a balanced perspective.

Advantages of Real Estate Investment Partnerships

1. *Shared Financial Burden:* One of the primary advantages of real estate investment partnerships is the ability to share the financial burden. By pooling capital from multiple partners, the partnership can access larger investment opportunities that may have been out of reach for individual investors. This shared financial responsibility allows partners to collectively invest in properties that have higher acquisition costs or require substantial renovations or maintenance.
2. *Diversified Expertise:* Real estate investment partnerships often bring together partners with diverse skill sets and expertise. Each partner may have a unique background in areas such as real estate development, property management, finance, or legal matters. This diverse knowledge pool allows for more comprehensive analysis, decision-making, and risk management. Partners can leverage each other's expertise to identify investment opportunities, conduct due diligence, negotiate deals, and manage properties more effectively.
3. *Access to Larger Investment Opportunities:* Through a real estate investment partnership, partners gain access to larger and potentially more lucrative investment opportunities. The combined financial resources and expertise of the partners can open doors to properties in prime locations, high-demand markets, or emerging real estate sectors. These opportunities may provide higher potential returns on investment compared to individual investments.
4. *Potential Tax Advantages:* Real estate investment partnerships can offer potential tax advantages. Partnerships are typically treated as pass-through entities for tax purposes, meaning that the partnership itself does not pay income taxes. Instead, profits and losses flow through to individual

partners, who report them on their personal tax returns. This structure can allow partners to take advantage of deductions, depreciation benefits, and other tax incentives related to real estate investments.

Disadvantages of Real Estate Investment Partnerships

1. *Decision-Making Complexities:* As real estate investment partnerships involve multiple partners, decision-making can become complex and time-consuming. Partners may have differing opinions, investment strategies, or risk appetites. Achieving consensus on property acquisitions, financing options, property management, or exit strategies can be challenging and may require extensive discussions and negotiations. The decision-making process may be slower compared to individual investments, which could impact the partnership's ability to capitalize on time-sensitive opportunities.
2. *Profit Sharing:* Profit sharing is a fundamental aspect of real estate investment partnerships. While it allows partners to distribute the rewards of their collective efforts, it can also become a potential source of conflict. Determining the appropriate distribution of profits can be subjective and may lead to disagreements among partners. It's important to establish clear and fair profit-sharing mechanisms in the partnership agreement to minimize disputes and maintain the partnership's stability.
3. *Potential Conflicts Among Partners:* Real estate investment partnerships may face conflicts arising from differences in opinions, goals, or expectations. Disagreements regarding investment strategies, property management decisions, or exit plans can strain the partnership's dynamics. Effective

communication, trust, and a well-defined dispute resolution process are essential to address and resolve conflicts in a constructive manner. It's important to choose partners who share a common vision and have compatible working styles and values to minimize potential conflicts.

4. *Limited Control and Autonomy:* Partners in a real estate investment partnership may have to compromise on individual control and autonomy. Decision-making processes, property management approaches, or investment strategies may require collective agreement or consensus. This shared decision-making structure may limit the flexibility and independence that individual investors enjoy. Partners must be willing to collaborate and align their objectives with the partnership's goals, accepting that certain decisions will be made collectively rather than individually.
5. *Dependency on Partner Performance in Real Estate Investment Partnerships:* Real estate investment partnerships rely on the active participation and performance of all partners. If one partner fails to fulfill their obligations or underperforms, it can negatively impact the partnership's overall success. Partners should conduct thorough due diligence when selecting potential partners to ensure they have a track record of reliability, competence, and commitment. Additionally, contingency plans should be in place to address situations where a partner may need to be replaced or withdraw from the partnership.

In summary, real estate investment partnerships offer both advantages and disadvantages that should be carefully considered. While they provide shared financial burden, diversified expertise, and access to larger investment opportunities, challenges such as decision-making complexities and potential conflicts among partners exist. To maximize the benefits and mitigate these challenges, establishing clear communication, trust, and shared goals is crucial. Thorough vetting of partners, conducting due diligence, and having a well-defined partnership agreement are essential. Ultimately, investors should weigh the pros and cons outlined in this section to determine if a real estate investment partnership aligns with their investment strategy and goals.

10.5 Establishing a Real Estate Investment Partnership:

Forming a real estate investment partnership requires careful planning and consideration of various factors. This section will provide guidance on the key steps and considerations involved in establishing a successful partnership.

1. Defining Partnership Roles and Responsibilities

To ensure a smooth operation, it's important to clearly define the roles and responsibilities of each partner within the partnership. This includes determining who will be responsible for *identifying potential investment opportunities*, *conducting due diligence*, *negotiating deals*, *managing properties*, *overseeing finances*, and *handling legal matters*. By assigning specific roles, partners can leverage their individual strengths and expertise, ensuring efficient decision-making and effective execution of tasks.

2. Setting Investment Goals and Strategies

Partners should establish clear investment goals and strategies that align with their collective vision. This includes defining the *types of properties to target* (residential, commercial, industrial), *desired locations*, *risk tolerance*, *expected returns*, and *investment timelines*. By setting specific investment criteria, partners can focus their efforts on opportunities that meet their predetermined objectives. Regularly reviewing and updating these goals and strategies can help adapt to changing market conditions and optimize investment performance.

3. Drafting a Partnership Agreement

A well-drafted partnership agreement is essential to *formalize the rights*, *responsibilities*, and *obligations* of each partner. The partnership agreement should cover various aspects, including the *purpose of the partnership*, *capital contributions from each partner*, *profit-sharing mechanisms*, *decision-making processes*, *dispute resolution procedures*, and *provisions for adding or removing partners*. It's advisable to consult with legal professionals experienced in real estate partnerships to ensure the agreement reflects the partners' intentions and provides a solid foundation for the partnership.

4. Establishing a Capital Contribution Plan

Partners must determine the capital contributions required from each member and establish a clear plan for making those contributions. This includes specifying the timing and *amounts of initial capital contributions* as well as *any subsequent contributions* for ongoing operational expenses or future investments. Partners should also consider how *additional capital needs* will be addressed, such as securing financing or attracting outside investors, if necessary. Clarity on capital contributions ensures transparency and equitable participation among partners.

5. Considering Exit Strategies

It's important to establish exit strategies within the partnership agreement to address potential circumstances where partners may wish to exit the partnership. Exit strategies can include options such as *selling their partnership interest* to other partners, *finding a new partner* to buy out their share, or *selling the entire portfolio of properties.* Defining the procedures for valuing the partnership interest and the process for transferring ownership ensures a smooth transition and minimizes potential conflicts when a partner decides to exit the partnership.

6. Maintaining Communication and Regular Review

Ongoing communication and regular partnership meetings are crucial for the success of a real estate investment partnership. Partners should establish a framework for regular communication to discuss investment opportunities, *property performance, financials*, and any other matters relevant to the partnership's success. Periodic reviews and evaluations of the partnership's performance and goals can help identify areas for improvement and make necessary adjustments to achieve long-term success.

In summary, establishing a real estate investment partnership requires careful planning, open communication, and a clear understanding of each partner's roles, responsibilities, and investment objectives. Defining partnership roles, setting investment goals and strategies, drafting a comprehensive partnership agreement, considering exit strategies, and maintaining regular communication are critical steps in forming a successful partnership. By following these guidelines, investors can leverage their collective resources, expertise, and capital to pursue profitable real estate ventures while mitigating risks and maximizing returns.

Conclusion

Real estate investment partnerships offer individuals and groups the opportunity to leverage their resources and expertise for profitable ventures in the real estate market. These partnerships provide advantages such as shared financial burden, access to larger opportunities, and diversified expertise. However, challenges like decision-making complexities and potential conflicts need to be addressed through clear communication, trust, and well-defined partnership agreements. Establishing roles, setting investment goals, and considering exit strategies are crucial steps in forming successful partnerships. By following these guidelines, investors can maximize the benefits of real estate investment partnerships and achieve shared success in the dynamic real estate market.

Chapter 11: Real Estate Financing for Flipping Houses

11.1 Understanding the Differences Between Financing for Flips and Financing for Rentals

Real estate investors employ various strategies to generate profits, with two popular approaches being house flipping and rental property ownership. While both strategies offer potential financial rewards, they require distinct financing considerations due to their differing natures. This section aims to shed light on the divergences between financing options for flips and rentals, providing readers with a comprehensive understanding of the unique characteristics and considerations associated with each investment strategy.

House Flipping Financing

House flipping refers to the practice of purchasing properties with the intention of renovating and reselling them for a profit within a relatively short period. This investment strategy requires quick access to funding and a keen eye for identifying undervalued properties. Here are some key points to consider regarding financing for flips:

1. Short-Term Financing Needs: Flips typically involve a shorter investment horizon compared to rentals. As such, house flippers often require financing options that cater to their *immediate capital needs.* Traditional mortgages may not be suitable due to their lengthy approval processes. Instead, house flippers often opt for alternative financing sources, such as *hard money loans* or *lines of credit*, which provide faster access to funds.

2. Higher Interest Rates and Fees: Given the higher risk associated with house flipping, lenders often charge higher interest rates and fees for short-term financing. Flippers should be prepared to absorb these additional costs when calculating their potential profits. It's essential to carefully evaluate the terms and costs of different financing options to ensure they align with the project's profitability goals.

3. Focus on Property Value and Renovation Plans: When seeking financing for flips, lenders primarily assess the *potential after-repair value (ARV)* of the property rather than the current market value. This valuation takes into account the estimated value of the property after renovations. Lenders will also scrutinize the flipper's renovation plans and budget to ensure they align with the property's value appreciation potential.

Rental Property Financing

Rental property investing involves purchasing properties with the intent of generating long-term income through rental payments. This strategy offers the potential for consistent cash flow and long-term appreciation. Here are some key considerations for financing rental properties:

1. Long-Term Financing Options: Unlike house flipping, rental property investors typically seek long-term financing options, such as traditional mortgages. These mortgages offer more *extended repayment periods*, often spanning 15 to 30 years, allowing investors to spread out their payments and generate positive cash flow from rental income.

2. Emphasis on Cash Flow and Rental Income: When securing financing for rental properties, lenders place significant importance on the property's cash flow potential. They evaluate factors such as market rental rates, vacancy rates, and the investor's ability to cover mortgage payments with rental income. Investors must provide detailed *financial projections* and demonstrate the property's ability to generate consistent cash flow.

3. Debt-to-Income (DTI) Ratios and Credit Scores: Lenders assessing rental property financing applications focus on the borrower's debt-to-income ratio and credit score. Since rental property investments carry long-term financial commitments, lenders scrutinize the investor's ability to manage multiple properties and debts. Maintaining a *healthy credit score* and *managing existing debts* are crucial for obtaining favorable rental property financing terms.

In summary, real estate investors must understand the distinctions between financing for flips and financing for rentals to maximize returns. Flipping houses requires quick funding access, often through alternative financing, while rental properties emphasize long-term cash flow and property management. Investors should select financing options aligned with their goals, considering interest rates, fees, renovation plans, and cash flow potential. Thorough research and professional advice are crucial before making financing decisions. Some investors may combine both strategies, necessitating considerations of overall investment strategy, available capital, and market conditions.

By understanding these differences, investors can make informed financing choices and excel in their real estate ventures.

11.2 Identifying Financing Options for Flipping Houses

Flipping houses can be a profitable real estate investment strategy, but it often requires financing to purchase and renovate properties *quickly*. In this section, we will explore the different financing options available for flipping houses, including both traditional and alternative options. Understanding these options can help investors make informed decisions and secure the necessary funds for their flipping projects.

Traditional Financing Options

Conventional Loans: Conventional loans, offered by banks and traditional lenders, are a common financing option for house flips. These loans typically have competitive interest rates and flexible terms. However, they often require a *good credit score*, a *low debt-to-income ratio*, and a *substantial down payment*. Conventional loans are suitable for investors with strong financial profiles and a track record of successful flips.

Alternative Financing Options

Hard Money Loans: Hard money loans are short-term loans provided by private lenders or investor groups. These loans are based on the value of the property being flipped rather than the borrower's creditworthiness. Hard money loans have higher interest rates and shorter repayment periods compared to conventional loans. They are ideal for investors who *may not qualify for traditional financing* or need quick access to funds for *time-sensitive opportunities*.

Private Money Loans: Private money loans are similar to hard money loans but are obtained from *individual investors* rather than institutional lenders. These loans offer flexibility in terms of repayment schedules and can be negotiated directly with the lender. Private money loans are suitable for investors who have established relationships with private lenders or have access to a network of potential investors.

Considerations and Eligibility Requirements

When considering financing options for flipping houses, investors should consider several factors:

Property Requirements: Different lenders may have specific property requirements, such as the property's condition, location, and potential after-repair value (ARV). Investors should ensure their chosen financing option aligns with the property they intend to flip.

Down Payment: Traditional financing options often require a *significant down payment*, while alternative options may have more flexible requirements. Investors should evaluate their available capital and choose a financing option that suits their financial capabilities.

Creditworthiness: Traditional loans typically require a good credit score, while alternative options focus more on the property's value and the investor's experience. Investors should assess their creditworthiness and explore financing options that align with their credit profile.

Speed and Flexibility: Flipping houses often requires quick access to funds, as opportunities may arise and need to be capitalized on swiftly. Alternative financing options such as hard money loans and private money loans offer *faster approval processes* and *greater flexibility* compared to traditional loans.

In summary, identifying the right financing options for flipping houses is crucial for real estate investors. Traditional financing options like conventional loans provide competitive rates for investors with strong financial profiles, while alternative options like hard money loans and private money loans offer flexibility and accessibility to those who may not qualify for traditional financing. By considering the property requirements, down payment capabilities, creditworthiness, and the need for speed and flexibility, investors can choose the financing option that best suits their flipping projects and maximize their chances of success.

11.3 The Importance of Having a Solid Business Plan for Flips

Flipping houses can be a lucrative real estate investment strategy, but it requires careful planning and execution. One crucial aspect of flipping houses is having a solid business plan in place. Lenders and investors typically require a well-documented plan that outlines the purchase price, renovation costs, anticipated selling price, and projected profit margin. In this section, we will explore the importance of having a solid business plan for flips and the key elements it should include.

1. **Market Research:** Conducting thorough market research is essential when creating a business plan for flipping houses. This involves analyzing the *local real estate market*, *identifying trends*, understanding *buyer preferences*, and assessing the *demand for renovated properties*. By understanding market dynamics, investors can make informed decisions regarding property selection, pricing strategies, and renovation choices.
2. **Accurate Expense Estimation:** A solid business plan for flips should include accurate estimates of renovation costs and other expenses. Investors need to carefully assess the *property's condition*, identify *necessary repairs or upgrades*, and *obtain*

quotes from contractors and suppliers. By accurately estimating expenses, investors can determine the profitability of the project and secure the necessary financing.

3. **Anticipated Selling Price:** A key component of the business plan is the anticipated selling price of the flipped property. Investors need to research *comparable sales in the area* to determine a realistic selling price. This involves analyzing *recent sales data* for similar properties that have undergone renovations. By setting a *competitive selling price*, investors can attract potential buyers and maximize their profit potential.
4. **Projected Profit Margin:** The business plan should include a projected profit margin, which is the difference between the purchase price, renovation costs, and the anticipated selling price. Investors need to assess the potential profit margin to ensure the flip is financially viable and aligns with their investment goals. A solid business plan demonstrates a clear understanding of the potential returns on investment.
5. **Viable Strategy:** A successful business plan for flips should outline a viable strategy for executing the project. This includes defining the *scope of work*, *establishing a timeline*, and coordinating with contractors and other professionals involved in the renovation process. By demonstrating a well-thought-out strategy, investors can instill confidence in lenders and attract potential partners or investors.

Having a solid business plan is not only crucial for securing financing but also for guiding the entire flipping process. It provides a roadmap for investors to follow and helps mitigate risks by thoroughly assessing potential challenges and opportunities. A well-documented business plan showcases the investor's professionalism, commitment, and understanding of the market, increasing the likelihood of success in the flipping venture.

11.4 How to Present Your Plan to Potential Lenders

When seeking financing for flipping houses, *presenting* a well-crafted and comprehensive business plan is essential to impress potential lenders. This section will provide valuable guidance on how to effectively present your business plan, covering important aspects that lenders consider when evaluating loan applications.

Preparing a Professional Loan Application

To begin, it is crucial to prepare a professional loan application that showcases your business plan in a clear and organized manner. This includes a *cover letter introducing yourself and the project*, a concise *summary of your business plan*, and supporting documents such as *financial statements*, *market research data*, and *contractor estimates*. Take the time to ensure that all documents are error-free and easy to read, presenting a professional image to lenders.

Showcasing Previous Experience and Track Record

If you have prior experience in flipping houses or real estate investments, make sure to highlight it in your presentation. Discuss your *track record of successful flips*, emphasizing your ability to execute similar projects and generate profits. This demonstrates your competence and reliability as an investor. If you are a beginner, focus on any transferable skills or relevant experiences that contribute to the success of the project, such as project management or construction knowledge.

Highlighting the Property's Potential Value and Market Demand

One of the key elements of your business plan is highlighting the potential value of the property you plan to flip. Provide a detailed description of the property's desirable features, such as location, size, and amenities. Emphasize the property's location in a high-demand area and explain how it aligns with current market trends. Support your claims with *market research data* and *comparable sales*, showing lenders the potential profitability of the project.

Addressing Potential Risks and Mitigation Strategies

It is important to address potential risks associated with your flipping project and demonstrate that you have mitigation strategies in place. Identify risks such as *construction delays*, *unexpected costs*, or *market fluctuations* and present your plans for mitigating these risks. Discuss your contingency plans, including alternative exit strategies or backup funding sources, to assure lenders that you have considered potential challenges and are prepared to handle them.

Presenting Realistic Financial Projections

As mentioned, lenders will want to see realistic and feasible financial projections for your flipping project. Provide estimated costs for acquiring and renovating the property, as well as an expected timeline for completion. Present your anticipated selling price and projected profit margin based on careful analysis and market trends. It is important to use *conservative estimates* and consider potential setbacks that may impact the project's profitability. This demonstrates your understanding of the financial aspects of the project and reassures lenders that you have accounted for potential risks.

In summary, effectively presenting your business plan to potential lenders is crucial for securing financing for flipping houses. By preparing a professional loan application, showcasing your experience and track record, highlighting the property's potential value and market demand, addressing potential risks, and presenting realistic financial projections, you can increase your chances of success. Remember to be prepared for questions and negotiations, and be open to adjustments that align with your goals. With a compelling business plan, you can demonstrate your expertise, preparedness, and potential for a profitable flipping project, ultimately attracting the necessary financing to bring your vision to life.

Conclusion

In conclusion, successfully financing and managing a house flipping project requires careful planning, thorough research, and effective financial management. By developing a solid business plan, selecting the right financing option, and implementing sound financial practices, investors can increase their chances of success. By combining these strategies, investors can navigate the house flipping market and achieve their financial goals in real estate.

Chapter 12: Financing Multifamily Properties

Multifamily properties are a popular investment option in the real estate market, providing opportunities for a steady income and potential appreciation. This section will provide an overview of some of the different types of multifamily properties, explaining the distinctions between duplexes, triplexes, apartment complexes, and other multifamily housing options. By understanding the various property types and their unique characteristics, readers will gain insights into the multifamily market and the different investment opportunities it presents.

12.1 The Different Types of Multi-Family Properties

Duplexes

A duplex is a type of multifamily property that consists of two separate residential units within a single building. Each unit typically has its own entrance, living space, kitchen, and bathroom. Duplexes are often sought after by both investors and owner-occupiers. They offer the advantage of generating rental income from one unit while allowing the owner to live in the other. Duplexes are commonly found in urban and suburban areas and are a suitable option for those looking for a smaller-scale multifamily investment.

Triplexes and Fourplexes

Triplexes and fourplexes are multifamily properties that consist of three and four separate residential units, respectively, within a single building. Similar to duplexes, each unit has its *own amenities and living space*. Triplexes and fourplexes provide investors with the opportunity to generate rental income from multiple units, while still offering the advantage of a relatively small-scale property. These types of properties are typically found in residential neighborhoods and can be an attractive option for investors looking for a slightly larger multifamily investment.

Apartment Complexes

Apartment complexes are *larger-scale multifamily properties* that consist of multiple residential units within a single building or a group of buildings. They can range in size from a few units to hundreds of units. Apartment complexes offer a wide range of amenities and are *typically managed by a property management company*. They are commonly found in urban areas and can cater to various tenant demographics, such as families, young professionals, or retirees. Investing in apartment complexes requires more extensive management and financial resources, but it also offers the potential for higher rental income and economies of scale.

Mixed-Use Developments

Mixed-use developments *combine residential units with commercial spaces*, such as retail shops, restaurants, or offices, within the same property. These developments aim to create a sense of community and convenience by providing residents with easy access to various amenities and services. Mixed-use developments can take the form of apartment buildings with ground-floor retail spaces or larger-scale projects that integrate multiple residential and commercial components. Investing in mixed-use developments requires careful consideration of both the residential and commercial aspects, as well as understanding the local market dynamics and demand for mixed-use properties.

Student Housing

Student housing is a specialized type of multifamily property that caters specifically to college or university students. These properties are strategically *located near educational institutions* and offer amenities and features tailored to student needs. Student housing can range from small houses or apartments to larger complexes with multiple units. Investing in student housing requires an understanding of the local student population, demand for off-campus housing, and the specific regulations and dynamics of the student housing market.

Understanding the different types of multifamily properties allows investors to identify the most suitable investment opportunities based on their investment goals, budget, and risk appetite. Factors such as property size, structure, tenant occupancy, location, and market demand all play a role in determining the potential returns and success of a multifamily investment. By carefully evaluating these factors and conducting thorough market research, investors can make informed decisions and maximize their chances of success in the multifamily real estate market.

12.2 Financing Options for Multifamily Properties

When it comes to investing in multifamily properties, securing the right financing is essential for success. Multifamily properties, which include apartment complexes and other residential buildings with multiple units, often require substantial capital to acquire or develop. This section will explore various financing options available to investors interested in multifamily properties. We will discuss traditional options like commercial mortgages as well as alternative options such as syndication and crowdfunding. Understanding the key features, eligibility requirements, and considerations of each financing option is crucial for making informed investment decisions in the multifamily real estate market.

Traditional Financing Options

Commercial Mortgages: Commercial mortgages are a common choice for financing multifamily properties. These loans are provided by banks, credit unions, or other financial institutions and are secured by the property itself. Commercial mortgages typically have *longer terms* compared to residential mortgages, ranging from 5 to 30 years. They can be either fixed-rate or adjustable-rate mortgages, offering flexibility for borrowers.

To qualify for a commercial mortgage, lenders assess factors such as the borrower's creditworthiness, property valuation, income potential, and the borrower's ability to make the required down payment. Generally, lenders require a down payment of at least 20-25% of the property's purchase price.

Alternative Financing Options

Syndication: Syndication is an alternative financing option where *multiple investors pool their resources* to acquire or develop multifamily properties. It involves forming a syndication company, which can take the form of a limited partnership (LP) or a limited liability company (LLC), and each investor contributes capital to the venture.

Syndication allows investors to access larger multifamily properties that may be beyond their individual financial means. It also provides an opportunity to *leverage the expertise and resources of multiple investors.* However, syndication requires careful structuring, legal documentation, and clear communication among the investors to ensure a smooth and successful investment venture.

Crowdfunding: Crowdfunding has gained popularity in recent years as a financing option for real estate investments, including multifamily properties. Crowdfunding platforms *connect individual investors with real estate projects*, allowing them to contribute smaller amounts of capital.

In the context of multifamily properties, crowdfunding platforms often offer opportunities to invest in specific projects or funds *managed by experienced professionals.* Investors can review project details, projected returns, and the track record of the project sponsors before making an investment decision.

Crowdfunding provides an accessible way for individual investors to *diversify their real estate portfolios* and access the multifamily market. However, investors should carefully evaluate the platform's credibility, the project's viability, and the associated fees and terms before committing their capital.

Considerations

When considering financing options for multifamily properties, several factors should be taken into account. These include the investor's financial position, creditworthiness, investment goals, and risk tolerance. Additionally, property location, market conditions, potential rental income, and long-term sustainability should also be considered when selecting a financing option.

It is crucial to consult with financial advisors, real estate professionals, and legal experts to **assess the suitability** of each financing option for specific investment scenarios. By understanding the key features, eligibility requirements, and considerations of each financing option, investors can make well-informed decisions and maximize their chances of success in the multifamily real estate market.

Investors should also consider the **repayment terms** and cash flow implications of each financing option. Commercial mortgages often come with regular monthly payments that include both principal and interest. It's essential to assess whether the projected rental income from the multifamily property will be sufficient to cover these expenses and generate positive cash flow.

In the case of **syndication**, investors should carefully review the terms of the partnership or LLC agreement. They should understand their rights and responsibilities as limited partners or members and have a clear understanding of how profits will be distributed. Additionally, investors should evaluate the experience and track record of the syndication company and its management team to ensure they have a strong reputation and a proven ability to generate returns.

For **crowdfunding** investments, investors should conduct thorough due diligence on the platform and the specific project before committing their funds. They should review the project's financial projections, market analysis, and the credentials of the project sponsors. It's also important to understand the liquidity of the investment and any potential fees or restrictions associated with withdrawing funds.

In summary, financing options for multifamily properties provide investors with diverse avenues to enter and thrive in the real estate market. Traditional options like commercial mortgages offer stability and favorable terms, while alternative options like syndication and crowdfunding provide opportunities for collaboration and access to a wider range of properties. By thoroughly understanding the features, eligibility requirements, and considerations of each financing option, investors can make informed decisions aligned with their investment goals and risk tolerance. Consulting with professionals and conducting comprehensive due diligence is crucial to mitigating risks and maximizing returns in the multifamily real estate sector.

12.3 How to Evaluate a Multifamily Property's Financials

Evaluating the financials of a multifamily property is a critical step in the investment process. It involves analyzing various aspects of the property's financial performance to determine its profitability and potential return on investment. This section will provide an overview of how to evaluate a multifamily property's financials, covering key areas such as rental income potential, operating expenses, cash flow analysis, and financial statement review. Understanding these factors will enable investors to make informed decisions and identify properties that align with their investment goals.

Assessing Rental Income Potential

One of the primary considerations when evaluating a multifamily property is the rental income potential. To assess this, investors should analyze factors such as the current rent roll, market rents in the area, and the property's occupancy rate. The following steps can help in the evaluation process:

1. *Rent Roll Analysis:* Review the property's rent roll, which provides a breakdown of the rents being collected from each unit. Assess the current rental rates and identify any units that are below market rents. This analysis helps in understanding the income potential of the property.
2. *Market Rent Comparison:* Research the local rental market to determine the average rents for similar properties in the area. This information helps in assessing whether the property's current rental rates are in line with market trends or if there is potential for rent increases.
3. Occupancy Rate: Evaluate the property's historical occupancy rate and compare it to the market average. A high occupancy rate indicates strong demand and stability, while a lower occupancy rate may require further investigation to understand the reasons behind it.

Analyzing Operating Expenses

Evaluating a multifamily property's operating expenses is crucial for understanding its financial viability. Investors should carefully review the property's expense history and consider the following factors:

1. *Fixed and Variable Expenses:* Identify the property's fixed expenses, such as property taxes, insurance, and utilities, which remain relatively stable over time. Variable expenses, such as maintenance and repairs, can vary based on the property's condition and age.
2. *Expense Ratio:* Calculate the property's expense ratio by

dividing the total operating expenses by the gross income. A lower expense ratio indicates better financial performance, as it suggests that a larger portion of the income is available for operating profit.

3. *Capital Expenditures:* Consider any anticipated capital expenditures, such as roof repairs or HVAC system replacements, which may impact the property's future cash flow. Assessing these expenses helps in determining the property's long-term sustainability and potential return on investment.

Conducting a Cash Flow Analysis

A comprehensive cash flow analysis is essential to evaluate the financial viability of a multifamily property. This analysis involves considering the property's rental income, operating expenses, debt service, and potential cash reserves. The following steps can guide investors in conducting a cash flow analysis:

1. *Gross Operating Income (GOI):* Calculate the GOI by subtracting vacancy losses and any other income adjustments from the total rental income. GOI represents the property's total income before deducting expenses.
2. *Net Operating Income (NOI):* Deduct the operating expenses from the GOI to calculate the NOI. This metric reflects the property's income after accounting for expenses but before considering debt service.
3. *Cash Flow Before Tax (CFBT):* Subtract the debt service (mortgage payment) from the NOI to determine the CFBT. This represents the cash flow generated by the property before considering taxes.
4. *Cash-on-Cash Return (CCR):* Calculate the CCR by dividing

the CFBT by the total cash investment (down payment and closing costs). The CCR provides insight into the property's return on investment based on the initial cash invested.

Reviewing Financial Statements

To gain a comprehensive understanding of a multifamily property's financials, investors should review the property's financial statements. These statements provide a detailed overview of the property's income, expenses, and overall financial health. Consider the following aspects when reviewing financial statements:

1. *Income Statement:* The income statement, also known as the profit and loss statement, summarizes the property's revenues and expenses over a specific period. It provides a snapshot of the property's financial performance and helps identify trends or areas that require further investigation.
2. *Balance Sheet:* The balance sheet provides a snapshot of the property's financial position at a specific point in time. It includes assets (such as the property itself and any cash reserves) and liabilities (such as outstanding mortgages or loans). Reviewing the balance sheet helps assess the property's overall financial stability and equity.
3. *Cash Flow Statement:* The cash flow statement tracks the inflows and outflows of cash for a specific period. It shows how cash is generated from rental income, operating activities, and financing activities, as well as how it is used for expenses, debt service, and investments. Analyzing the cash flow statement helps assess the property's cash management and liquidity.
4. *Capitalization Rate:* The capitalization rate, or cap rate, is a key metric used in real estate valuation. It measures the

property's net operating income (NOI) as a percentage of its market value or purchase price. Reviewing the cap rate provides insight into the property's income potential and its value relative to similar properties in the market.

Evaluating a multifamily property's financials is a crucial step in the investment process. By assessing the rental income potential, analyzing operating expenses, conducting a cash flow analysis, and reviewing financial statements, investors can gain a comprehensive understanding of the property's financial viability. Key metrics such as NOI, cap rate, and cash-on-cash return help in assessing the property's potential return on investment and profitability. It is essential to conduct thorough due diligence and consult with professionals to ensure accurate evaluation and informed investment decisions in the multifamily real estate market.

12.4 The Role of Property Management in Multifamily Financing

Property management plays a crucial role in the success of multifamily financing. Effective property management ensures that multifamily properties are well-maintained, attract quality tenants, and generate steady income. This section explores the significance of property management in multifamily financing, emphasizing its impact on income generation, tenant satisfaction, and overall financial performance.

Maximizing Income Generation

One of the primary roles of property management in multifamily financing is to maximize income generation. A well-managed property *attracts tenants* and *maintains high occupancy rates*, resulting in a steady stream of rental income. Property managers are responsible for setting *competitive rental rates, conducting thorough tenant screenings*, and *implementing effective marketing strategies* to attract prospective renters. Additionally, they ensure timely rent collection and handle any tenant-related issues or disputes promptly. By effectively managing these aspects, property managers can optimize the property's income potential and enhance its financial performance.

Enhancing Tenant Satisfaction

Property management also plays a vital role in ensuring tenant satisfaction, which is crucial for tenant retention and attracting new tenants through positive word-of-mouth. Property managers are responsible for maintaining the property's *physical condition*, promptly addressing *maintenance and repair issues*, and providing a *safe and comfortable living environment* for residents. They also handle tenant requests and concerns, ensuring effective communication and timely resolution of issues. By prioritizing tenant satisfaction, property managers can foster a positive living experience for residents, leading to higher tenant retention rates and a positive reputation for the property.

Mitigating Financial Risks

Effective property management is essential in mitigating financial risks associated with multifamily properties. Property managers monitor the *property's financial performance*, including expenses, cash flow, and budgeting. They identify *cost-saving opportunities*, negotiate contracts with vendors, and implement *efficient operational processes to minimize expenses*. Additionally, property managers conduct regular inspections to identify and address potential risks, such as safety hazards or property damage. By proactively managing financial aspects and mitigating risks, property managers safeguard the property's profitability and protect the interests of investors and stakeholders.

Maximizing Returns on Investment

Property management significantly impacts the overall financial performance and returns on investment for multifamily properties. A well-managed property *attracts quality tenants, maintains high occupancy rates*, and *generates steady rental income*. Property managers conduct *regular market analyses* to stay updated on rental trends and adjust rental rates accordingly. They also implement strategies to *optimize operating efficiencies, reduce vacancies*, and *minimize turnover costs*. By focusing on maximizing the property's income potential and controlling expenses, property managers can enhance the property's net operating income (NOI) and overall return on investment (ROI).

In multifamily financing, property management plays a crucial role in maximizing income generation, enhancing tenant satisfaction, mitigating financial risks, and maximizing returns on investment. Effective property management ensures that multifamily properties operate smoothly, attracting quality tenants and generating steady rental income. By maintaining the property's physical condition, addressing tenant concerns, and implementing cost-saving measures, property managers contribute to the property's financial success. Investors and stakeholders who understand the importance of property management can make informed decisions to optimize the potential returns and mitigate risks associated with multifamily properties.

12.5 Tips for Successful Multifamily Financing

Navigating the multifamily financing landscape requires careful planning and strategic decision-making. This section offers practical tips that can help investors and stakeholders achieve successful multifamily financing. From building strong relationships with lenders to staying updated on market trends, implementing these strategies can contribute to a smooth and prosperous financing process.

Build Relationships with Lenders

Establishing strong relationships with lenders is vital for successful multifamily financing. It is important to research and identify lenders who *specialize in multifamily properties* and have a *proven track record* in the industry. Building rapport with these lenders through networking events, industry conferences, and personal introductions can enhance credibility and increase the chances of obtaining favorable financing terms. Maintaining open lines of communication and demonstrating a solid understanding of the property's financials and business plan will further strengthen these relationships.

Conduct Thorough Due Diligence

Thorough due diligence is crucial when pursuing multifamily financing. Before committing to a property, investors should conduct a comprehensive analysis of its *financials*, *market conditions*, and *potential risks*. This includes reviewing historical financial records, evaluating the property's physical condition, assessing market demand and rental trends, and analyzing the competition. Engaging professionals such as real estate attorneys, appraisers, and property inspectors can provide valuable insights during the due diligence process, helping to identify any red flags or potential issues that could impact financing.

Assemble a Strong Team of Professionals

A successful multifamily financing endeavor requires a strong team of professionals. Engaging experts who specialize in multifamily properties, such as *real estate brokers*, *property managers*, and *financial advisors*, can provide invaluable guidance and expertise. These professionals can assist with *property valuation*, *market analysis*, *financial projections*, and *navigating the financing process*. Collaborating with a skilled team ensures that all aspects of the multifamily financing journey are handled efficiently and effectively.

Maintain Accurate Financial Records

Accurate financial records are essential for successful multifamily financing. Investors should establish robust accounting systems and maintain meticulous records of income, expenses, and cash flow. Lenders will scrutinize these financial records during the underwriting process to assess the property's financial performance and evaluate its financing eligibility. By maintaining accurate and up-to-date financial records, investors can *present a clear and transparent financial picture* to lenders, increasing their confidence in the investment.

Stay Updated on Market Trends

Staying informed about market trends is vital for successful multifamily financing. Investors should regularly monitor *rental market conditions*, *vacancy rates*, *rental price trends*, and *local economic factors* that may impact the property's performance. This information helps investors make informed decisions regarding *rental rates*, *financing terms*, and *investment strategies*. By staying updated on market trends, investors can proactively adapt their financing plans to align with current market conditions and maximize their investment returns.

Achieving successful multifamily financing requires a combination of strategic planning, thorough due diligence, and informed decision-making. Building strong relationships with lenders, conducting thorough due diligence, assembling a skilled team of professionals, maintaining accurate financial records, and staying updated on market trends are essential strategies for navigating the multifamily financing landscape. By implementing these tips, investors and stakeholders can increase their chances of securing favorable financing terms, optimizing the property's financial performance, and achieving long-term success in multifamily real estate investments.

Conclusion

In summary, financing multifamily properties requires a thorough understanding of the property types, financial evaluation, property management, and effective financing strategies. By carefully evaluating property dynamics, conducting financial due diligence, prioritizing property management, and implementing strategic financing approaches, investors can position themselves for success in the multifamily market. With a comprehensive understanding and the right strategies in place, investors can maximize their chances of achieving their financial goals in the multifamily sector.

Chapter 13: Financing for Commercial Real Estate

Commercial Leasehold Investing - Photo by Sean Pollock

13.1 Understanding the Different Types of Commercial Real Estate

Commercial real estate encompasses a wide range of property types, each serving different purposes and attracting distinct tenant profiles. This section aims to provide an overview of the various types of commercial real estate properties, highlighting their unique characteristics and market dynamics. By understanding these property categories, readers can gain valuable insights into the diverse opportunities and considerations associated with commercial real estate investments.

Office Buildings

Office buildings are commercial properties designed to accommodate businesses and professional services. They range from small *suburban office parks* to *large downtown high-rises*. Office buildings are typically leased to tenants for the purpose of conducting administrative, managerial, or professional operations. They often feature amenities such as conference rooms, common areas, and parking facilities. The demand for office space is influenced by factors such as local job growth, economic conditions, and the overall business climate.

Retail Centers

Retail centers encompass a variety of commercial properties that house retail businesses. These can include *strip malls*, *shopping centers*, and *regional malls*. Retail centers are leased to tenants who operate businesses such as clothing stores, restaurants, grocery stores, and entertainment venues. The success of retail centers depends on factors such as location, foot traffic, demographics, and consumer spending patterns. Retail properties are often affected by shifts in consumer preferences, e-commerce trends, and overall economic conditions.

Industrial Warehouses

Industrial warehouses are commercial properties designed for *manufacturing, production, storage*, and *distribution purposes*. They can range from *small industrial parks* to *large distribution centers*. Industrial warehouses often feature high ceilings, loading docks, and ample storage space. Tenants of industrial properties include manufacturers, logistics companies, wholesalers, and e-commerce businesses. The demand for industrial space is influenced by factors such as proximity to transportation infrastructure, supply chain needs, and economic growth.

Hospitality Properties

Hospitality properties, such as *hotels*, *resorts*, and *vacation rentals*, cater to temporary accommodation needs for travelers and tourists. These properties offer amenities and services such as rooms, restaurants, event spaces, and recreational facilities. The success of hospitality properties is closely tied to factors such as tourism trends, travel demand, location, and the overall hospitality market. Investors in hospitality properties must consider factors such as seasonality, market saturation, and competition from alternative accommodation options.

Commercial real estate encompasses a diverse range of property types, each serving different purposes and attracting distinct tenant profiles. Understanding the distinctions between office buildings, retail centers, industrial warehouses, multifamily properties, and hospitality properties is crucial for investors and stakeholders in the commercial real estate industry. By recognizing the unique characteristics and market dynamics associated with each property type, investors can make informed decisions and capitalize on the opportunities available in the commercial real estate market.

13.2 Identifying Financing Options for Commercial Real Estate

When it comes to financing commercial real estate investments, there are various options available to investors and property owners. This section aims to explore the different financing options for commercial real estate, including both traditional and alternative methods. By understanding the key features, eligibility requirements, and considerations of each financing option, readers can make informed decisions regarding their commercial real estate financing needs.

Commercial Mortgages

Commercial mortgages are one of the most common and traditional financing options for commercial real estate. These loans are provided by banks, credit unions, and other financial institutions. Commercial mortgages are used to finance the acquisition or refinance of commercial properties. They typically have fixed or variable interest rates, amortization periods, and repayment terms ranging from 5 to 30 years. Eligibility requirements for commercial mortgages include a *strong credit history*, a *solid business plan*, a *down payment* (usually 20-30%), and *proof of property cash flow*.

Construction Loans

For investors looking to develop or renovate commercial properties, construction loans are a suitable financing option. These loans provide funding for the construction or renovation of commercial buildings, including office spaces, retail centers, and industrial warehouses. Construction loans typically have a *short-term duration* and are *disbursed in stages* as the project progresses. Interest rates on construction loans are often higher than those for commercial mortgages. Lenders evaluate the project's feasibility, the borrower's experience, and the property's potential value when determining eligibility for construction loans.

Small Business Administration (SBA) Loans

The Small Business Administration (SBA) offers financing options for small businesses seeking to acquire or expand commercial real estate. SBA loans provide longer repayment terms and lower down payment requirements compared to traditional commercial mortgages. The SBA guarantees a portion of the loan, reducing the risk for lenders. SBA 7(a) loans and SBA 504 loans are popular programs for commercial real estate financing. These loans have specific eligibility criteria, including a good credit score, a feasible business plan, and adherence to SBA size standards.

Mezzanine Financing

Mezzanine financing is a form of debt financing that *sits between senior debt (commercial mortgage) and equity in the capital structure*. It is often used to bridge the gap between the primary loan and the equity contribution in a commercial real estate project. Mezzanine loans have higher interest rates and typically involve *collateralizing the ownership interest in the property*. Mezzanine financing is commonly used for large-scale projects, such as *commercial developments or acquisitions*, and requires a thorough evaluation of the property's potential cash flow and the borrower's creditworthiness.

Commercial Real Estate Crowdfunding

Commercial real estate crowdfunding has emerged as an alternative financing option in recent years. It involves *pooling funds from multiple investors* to finance commercial real estate projects. Crowdfunding platforms allow individual investors to participate in real estate investments with lower capital requirements. Investors can choose from different projects and investment structures, such as debt or equity investments. However, it's essential to conduct thorough due diligence on the crowdfunding platform, the project sponsor, and the specific investment opportunity before committing funds.

Identifying the right financing option is crucial for successful commercial real estate investments. Traditional options such as commercial mortgages, construction loans, and SBA loans offer established and reliable paths for financing. Mezzanine financing and commercial real estate crowdfunding provide alternative avenues for investors seeking additional flexibility or access to diverse investment opportunities. Understanding the key features, eligibility requirements, and considerations of each financing option allows investors to make informed decisions that align with their commercial real estate financing needs and overall investment strategies.

13.3 The Importance of Due Diligence in Commercial Real Estate Financing

Conducting thorough due diligence is a critical step in commercial real estate financing. It involves evaluating various aspects of the property, market conditions, and financial performance to assess the investment's viability and mitigate potential risks. This section emphasizes the significance of due diligence in commercial real estate financing and highlights key areas that investors should focus on during this process.

Property Location and Market Assessment

One of the fundamental aspects of due diligence in commercial real estate financing is evaluating the property's *location and its market dynamics*. Assessing the property's proximity to transportation hubs, population centers, amenities, and infrastructure is crucial. Additionally, analyzing *market trends*, *supply and demand dynamics*, and *demographic* factors helps investors understand the property's potential for generating income and attracting tenants. A thorough understanding of the market conditions allows investors to gauge the property's long-term viability and potential for appreciation.

Financial Performance Evaluation

Evaluating the property's financial performance is an integral part of due diligence. This includes reviewing historical financial statements, rent rolls, and operating expenses to assess the property's income generation and profitability. Key financial metrics such as *net operating income (NOI)*, *cash flow*, and *capitalization rate* (cap rate) provide insights into the property's financial health and potential returns. Investors should also analyze *lease agreements*, *tenant profiles*, and *occupancy rates* to gauge stability and potential risks. Understanding the property's financial performance is crucial for determining its financing eligibility and projecting future cash flows.

Potential Risks and Legal Considerations

Assessing potential risks and legal considerations is an essential aspect of due diligence. Investors should identify and evaluate factors that could affect the property's value or introduce liabilities. This includes analyzing *environmental assessments*, *zoning and land use regulations*, *property condition* assessments, and potential *legal disputes*. Engaging professionals such as real estate attorneys, environmental consultants, and property inspectors can provide valuable insights and help identify any red flags or issues that may impact the financing process.

Property Condition and Physical Inspections

Conducting thorough *physical inspections* of the property is vital to assess its condition and identify any maintenance or repair needs. This includes inspecting the building's structure, mechanical systems, electrical systems, plumbing, and overall maintenance. Understanding the property's physical condition helps investors estimate potential capital expenditures and factor them into the financing and investment plans. Property inspections are typically performed by *professional inspectors* who specialize in commercial real estate.

Professional Team Engagement

Engaging a professional team is crucial to conduct a comprehensive due diligence process. Collaborating with experts such as *real estate attorneys*, *appraisers*, *property inspectors*, and *financial advisors* provides specialized knowledge and expertise. These professionals can help identify potential risks, evaluate the property's financials, and navigate the legal and regulatory aspects of commercial real estate financing. Leveraging the knowledge and experience of a skilled team contributes to a thorough and effective due diligence process.

Conducting due diligence in commercial real estate financing is of paramount importance. Thoroughly evaluating the property's location, market demand, financial performance, potential risks, and legal considerations provides investors with the necessary information to make informed decisions. By performing comprehensive due diligence, investors can assess the property's financial viability, identify potential risks, and align financing terms with the property's unique characteristics.

13.4 Creating a Comprehensive Business Plan for Commercial Real Estate

When seeking financing for commercial real estate investments, having a well-crafted and comprehensive business plan is essential. Lenders and investors require a thorough understanding of the property, its financial potential, and the strategies in place to generate income and achieve investment goals. This section highlights the importance of creating a comprehensive business plan for commercial real estate financing and explores the key components and considerations involved.

Property Details and Investment Summary

The first component of a comprehensive business plan is a *detailed description of the property* and an *investment summary*. This includes providing information about the property's location, size, type, and amenities. It also involves highlighting *the investment's purpose*, whether it is an *acquisition*, *development*, or *renovation*. Investors should outline the property's *unique selling points*, *market demand*, and *competitive advantages*. The investment summary should clearly communicate the financial goals, *return on investment (ROI)* expectations, and the *timeline for achieving those goals*.

Financial Projections and Analysis

Financial projections and analysis play a crucial role in a commercial real estate business plan. Investors need to present a *comprehensive financial forecast*, including projected income, expenses, cash flow, and profitability. This involves estimating rental income based on market rates, factoring in vacancy rates and potential rent escalations, and considering operating expenses such as property management, maintenance, insurance, and taxes. Investors should also include a *capital expenditure plan*, outlining any anticipated costs for property improvements or renovations. Financial analysis should demonstrate the property's ability to generate positive cash flow and provide a return on investment.

Market Analysis and Competitive Landscape

An in-depth market analysis is a vital component of a business plan for commercial real estate financing. This involves researching and understanding the *local market conditions*, *trends*, and *competitive landscape*. Investors should evaluate factors such as population growth, employment rates, economic indicators, and market demand for the property type. It is essential to *assess the supply and demand dynamics*, *rental rates*, and *occupancy levels* in the market. Identifying the target tenant base and understanding their preferences and needs is also crucial. A comprehensive market analysis helps lenders and investors assess the property's potential success and alignment with market trends.

Risk Assessment and Mitigation Strategies

Another important aspect of a comprehensive business plan is a thorough risk assessment and the inclusion of mitigation strategies. Investors should identify and evaluate potential risks that may impact the investment's success. This can include *market volatility*, *changes in economic conditions*, *regulatory changes*, *competitio*n, and *property-specific risks* such as environmental concerns or tenant defaults. Investors should outline risk mitigation strategies such as *contingency plans*, *insurance coverage*, *diversification*, and *property management protocols*. Demonstrating a clear understanding of potential risks and having strategies in place to mitigate them enhances the credibility and viability of the business plan.

Clear Strategy and Execution Plan

A comprehensive business plan should include a clear strategy for achieving investment goals and a well-defined execution plan. This involves *outlining the steps and milestones* for *property acquisition*, *development*, or *renovation*. Investors should detail the marketing and leasing strategy, including *tenant acquisition plans* and *lease-up projections*. It is important to demonstrate a thorough understanding of the property's operational and management requirements, including property management selection and ongoing maintenance plans. A well-crafted execution plan helps lenders and investors visualize the investor's commitment and ability to implement the strategies outlined in the business plan.

A comprehensive business plan is essential when seeking financing for commercial real estate investments. It demonstrates the investor's understanding of the property and market, showcases their expertise and commitment, and provides a roadmap for successful investment. A well-structured business plan increases the likelihood of securing financing, facilitates communication with stakeholders, and serves as a reference for decision-making and progress evaluation. Regular updates to the business plan ensure its relevance as the investment progresses. Overall, a comprehensive business plan is a vital tool in the commercial real estate financing process.

13.5 Building Relationships with Potential Lenders for Commercial Real Estate

Establishing strong relationships with potential lenders is crucial for securing favorable financing terms in commercial real estate. Building trust, rapport, and credibility with lenders enhances the investor's chances of obtaining financing and creates a foundation for successful long-term partnerships. This section provides guidance on building relationships with potential lenders and outlines effective strategies for networking, professional engagement, and preparedness.

Networking and Industry Involvement

Networking is a key strategy for building relationships with potential lenders in commercial real estate. Investors should actively engage in *industry events*, *conferences*, and *trade associations* to connect with lenders and other professionals in the field. Attending *networking events*, participating in *panel discussions*, and seeking opportunities for meaningful conversations with lenders can help establish initial connections. Building a strong professional network in the industry increases visibility, provides access to potential lenders, and opens doors to valuable insights and opportunities.

Seeking Referrals and Recommendations

Referrals and recommendations can be powerful tools for building relationships with lenders. Investors should leverage their existing network and *seek recommendations from trusted industry professionals*, including *real estate brokers*, *attorneys*, and *fellow investors*. Referrals from credible sources can help establish credibility and increase the likelihood of lenders considering financing requests. It is essential to nurture and maintain strong relationships with industry contacts who can vouch for the investor's track record, integrity, and ability to execute successful commercial real estate projects.

Approaching Lenders with Professionalism and Preparedness

When approaching potential lenders, professionalism and preparedness are key. Investors should conduct thorough research on prospective lenders, understand their lending criteria, and tailor their approach accordingly. This involves preparing a concise and well-presented *financing proposal* that clearly communicates the investment opportunity, the investor's financial strength, and the proposed terms of the loan. Providing *accurate and up-to-date financial information*, property details, and market analysis demonstrates professionalism and preparedness, which can significantly impact lenders' perception of the investor's credibility.

Building Trust and Rapport

Building trust and rapport with potential lenders is essential for long-term success in commercial real estate financing. Investors should strive to establish open and transparent communication with lenders, showcasing *integrity*, *honesty*, and a *commitment* to mutually beneficial partnerships. Regular updates on the progress of projects, timely responses to inquiries, and a willingness to address concerns contribute to building trust. Additionally, maintaining a track record of successful projects, meeting financial obligations, and delivering on promises strengthens lenders' confidence in the investor's capabilities.

Cultivating Long-Term Relationships

Commercial real estate financing is often a long-term endeavor, requiring ongoing relationships with lenders. Investors should view the lender relationship as a *partnership* and seek to *cultivate long-term connections*. This involves regular communication, providing updates on investment performance, and proactively addressing any issues or concerns. Building a positive and collaborative relationship with lenders can lead to repeat financing opportunities, access to additional capital, and potential introductions to other industry professionals.

Building relationships with potential lenders is a critical component of successful commercial real estate financing. By networking, seeking referrals, approaching lenders with professionalism and preparedness, and cultivating trust and rapport, investors can enhance their chances of securing favorable financing terms. Building strong relationships with lenders creates a foundation for long-term partnerships and increases the likelihood of accessing financing for future projects. Investors should prioritize establishing credibility, demonstrating integrity, and nurturing ongoing connections with lenders to maximize their opportunities in the commercial real estate market.

Conclusion

In summary, financing commercial real estate necessitates a thorough understanding of the market, available options, due diligence, business planning, and relationship building. By incorporating these elements, investors can navigate the complexities of commercial real estate financing with confidence. Understanding property types, exploring financing options, conducting due diligence, and creating a comprehensive business plan are essential steps. Building strong relationships with lenders also plays a crucial role. By embracing these strategies, investors can increase their chances of success in commercial real estate financing and maximize their investment potential.

Chapter 14: Creative Real Estate Financing Strategies

14.1 House Hacking: Maximizing Income through Real Estate Investment

House hacking has become an increasingly popular strategy for individuals seeking to generate additional income while simultaneously reducing their living expenses. This innovative approach to real estate investment involves living in a property and renting out a portion of it to tenants. By doing so, homeowners can offset their mortgage payments and potentially turn their living space into a profitable asset. In this section, we will delve into the concept of house hacking and explore how it offers financial advantages and a path to real estate investment.

Understanding House Hacking

House hacking involves purchasing a property with the intention of living in it while simultaneously renting out a part of it to tenants.

This could be done by renting out a *basement*, an *extra room*, a *garage apartment*, or even *dividing the property into separate units*. The income generated from renting out these spaces can be used to offset the mortgage, thus reducing the homeowner's monthly housing expenses.

Offsetting Mortgage Payments

One of the primary benefits of house hacking is the ability to offset mortgage payments. By renting out a portion of their property, homeowners can generate a steady stream of rental income that can be put towards their mortgage. In some cases, the rental income *may cover the entire mortgage*, effectively allowing the homeowner to live in the property for free. This can significantly reduce the financial burden associated with homeownership and provide individuals with greater flexibility in managing their finances.

Reduced Living Expenses

House hacking offers an opportunity to significantly reduce living expenses. By having tenants contribute to the mortgage payment, homeowners can free up a substantial portion of their income that would have otherwise gone towards housing costs. This can provide individuals with the *financial freedom* to invest in other areas or save for future goals. Moreover, by sharing living space with tenants, homeowners can also benefit from *shared utilities and maintenance expenses*, further reducing their overall living costs.

Real Estate Investment Opportunity

House hacking not only provides a means to offset housing expenses but also serves as a stepping stone toward real estate investment. By acquiring a property with multiple rental units, homeowners can start building their real estate portfolio without the need for substantial upfront capital. The rental income generated from house hacking can be used to *fund future real estate investments* or be reinvested into the current property, enhancing its value and potential rental income. Over time, homeowners can accumulate multiple properties and create a sustainable passive income stream.

House hacking offers a unique and financially advantageous approach to real estate investment. By renting out a portion of their property, homeowners can offset mortgage payments and significantly reduce their living expenses. This strategy not only provides immediate financial benefits but also serves as a stepping stone toward building a real estate portfolio. House hacking allows individuals to enter the real estate market with reduced living costs, providing a solid foundation for long-term wealth accumulation. Whether you're a first-time homebuyer or an experienced investor, exploring the concept of house hacking can be a wise financial decision.

14.2 BRRRR Method: Building a Real Estate Portfolio through Strategic Investment

The BRRRR method, an acronym for *Buy, Rehab, Rent, Refinance, Repeat*, is a popular strategy used by real estate investors to acquire and finance investment properties. This method allows investors to maximize their returns by leveraging the potential of distressed properties and creating a sustainable cash flow. In this section, we will explore the step-by-step process of the BRRRR method and highlight the benefits it offers to savvy investors.

Step 1: Buying Distressed Properties

The first step in the BRRRR method is to identify and purchase distressed properties. These properties are typically undervalued, *in need of repairs or renovations*, or facing financial distress. Investors can find distressed properties through various channels such as foreclosure listings, auctions, or working with real estate agents specializing in investment properties. The key is to conduct thorough research and due diligence to ensure the property's potential for profitability and future value appreciation.

Step 2: Rehabilitating the Property

Once the distressed property is acquired, the next step is to rehabilitate or renovate it to increase its value and attract potential tenants. Investors should create a budget and a detailed renovation plan to address any structural or cosmetic issues, making the property more appealing and marketable. The goal is to strike a balance between maximizing the property's value and keeping renovation costs reasonable to ensure a profitable investment.

Step 3: Renting Out the Property

After completing the necessary renovations, the property is ready to be rented out. Investors should conduct thorough market research to determine the *optimal rental price* and *attract reliable tenants*. Proper tenant screening is crucial to ensure timely rent payments and maintain the property's condition. By renting out the property, investors generate a steady rental income that contributes to the property's cash flow and covers ongoing expenses.

Step 4: Refinancing to Pull Out Invested Capital

Once the property is rented and generating income, investors can explore the option of refinancing. Refinancing involves replacing the existing mortgage with a new one, based on the *property's increased value*. By refinancing, investors can pull out a portion of the equity they have built through the property's appreciation and rental income. This allows them to recover their initial investment and use those funds to repeat the BRRRR process with another property.

Step 5: Repeating the Process

The final step in the BRRRR method is to repeat the process with additional investment properties. By refinancing and pulling out invested capital from the initial property, investors can use those funds to acquire and rehabilitate new properties. This iterative approach enables investors to build a portfolio of income-generating properties while minimizing their out-of-pocket expenses.

Summary

The BRRRR method provides a systematic and profitable approach to real estate investment. By strategically acquiring distressed properties, rehabilitating them, renting them out, refinancing to pull out invested capital, and repeating the process, investors can rapidly build a real estate portfolio and generate a sustainable cash flow. This method offers the potential for long-term wealth accumulation, leveraging the power of real estate and strategic financing.

14.3 Seller Financing: Unlocking Opportunities for Buyers and Sellers

Seller financing is an alternative method of financing a real estate transaction where the property seller acts as the lender, providing financing options to the buyer. In this arrangement, the buyer makes regular payments to the seller, usually in the form of a mortgage, instead of obtaining a traditional loan from a financial institution. In this section, we will explore the concept of seller financing, highlighting the benefits it offers to both buyers and sellers and the flexibility of terms that can be negotiated in such agreements.

Benefits for Buyers

Seller financing opens up opportunities for buyers who may face challenges obtaining traditional financing through banks or other lending institutions. This option allows buyers with *less-than-perfect credit scores*, *self-employed individuals*, or those with limited down payment funds to still purchase a property. Seller financing often has more flexible qualification requirements, making homeownership a possibility for a broader range of buyers. Additionally, buyers may avoid some of the closing costs associated with traditional loans, further reducing their upfront expenses.

Benefits for Sellers

Seller financing can be an attractive option for sellers looking to *sell their property quickly* and *generate income from the sale.* By offering financing to buyers, sellers expand the pool of potential buyers, as they can attract those who may not qualify for traditional financing. This *increased buyer pool* can lead to a faster sale, enabling sellers to move on to their next venture or investment. Additionally, sellers who act as lenders can earn interest on the loan, providing them with a steady stream of income over time.

Flexibility of Terms

One of the key advantages of seller financing is the flexibility it offers in negotiating terms. Buyers and sellers can work together to establish a *mutually beneficial agreement* that suits their specific needs. This flexibility extends to the *down payment amount*, *interest rate*, *repayment period*, and other terms of the loan. For example, sellers may be willing to accept a lower down payment, offer a competitive interest rate, or even negotiate a balloon payment at the end of the loan term. This customization allows both parties to tailor the agreement to their financial situation and goals.

Mitigating Risks

While seller financing presents opportunities, it is important for both buyers and sellers to carefully consider and mitigate potential risks. Sellers should conduct thorough due diligence on the buyer's financial capacity and creditworthiness to minimize the risk of default. Buyers should ensure they can comfortably meet the repayment obligations and carefully review the terms of the agreement. Legal assistance may be advisable to ensure the transaction adheres to local regulations and to protect the interests of both parties.

Seller financing offers a viable alternative to traditional financing methods, providing opportunities for both buyers and sellers in the real estate market. Buyers benefit from increased access to homeownership, even with limited credit or down payment options. Sellers can expedite property sales and generate income while potentially earning interest on the loan. The flexibility of terms allows for personalized agreements that meet the specific needs of both parties. When approached with caution and proper due diligence, seller financing can be a win-win solution in real estate transactions.

14.4 Subject-To Financing: Navigating Opportunities and Risks in Real Estate Transactions

Subject-to financing is a real estate strategy where a buyer acquires a property by taking over the existing mortgage without formally assuming the loan. In this arrangement, the buyer assumes responsibility for making mortgage payments, while the seller's name remains on the loan. In this section, we will delve into the concept of subject-to financing, examining its benefits, risks, and the importance of understanding the legal and financial implications involved.

The Basics of Subject-To Financing

Subject-to-financing allows buyers to acquire a property without having to secure a new loan or meet stringent financing requirements. The buyer purchases the property, and the *deed is transferred to the buyer*, but the *existing mortgage remains in the seller's name*. The buyer then *makes the mortgage payments directly to the lender*, effectively taking over the loan while the seller retains legal ownership of the property. This strategy can be particularly appealing when interest rates are low or when the buyer faces challenges in obtaining traditional financing.

Benefits of Subject-To Financing

Subject-to financing offers several potential benefits for both buyers and sellers. For buyers, this approach can provide an opportunity to acquire a property without the need for a substantial down payment or the costs associated with obtaining a new loan. It can be especially beneficial for buyers with limited credit history or those who do not meet traditional lending criteria. Sellers, on the other hand, can benefit from a *faster sale* and the ability to offload a property without going through the formal loan assumption process or incurring prepayment penalties.

Risks and Considerations

While subject-to-financing presents opportunities, it also carries risks and considerations that both buyers and sellers should be aware of. Buyers must understand that *they are taking on the responsibility of making mortgage payments*, and any default can have serious consequences, including foreclosure. Additionally, the seller's financial situation, such as late payments or default on the mortgage, can *impact the buyer's ability to continue making payments*. Both parties should conduct thorough due diligence, including reviewing the existing mortgage terms, assessing the property's value, and understanding the legal and financial implications of subject-to financing.

Legal and Financial Implications

Subject-to-financing involves legal and financial complexities that require careful consideration. Buyers and sellers should *seek professional advice*, such as legal counsel and real estate professionals, to navigate the transaction successfully. Understanding the legal requirements, including the necessity of a *well-drafted purchase agreement* and the potential *impact on the seller's credit*, is crucial. Buyers should also be prepared to handle potential challenges, such as loan acceleration clauses that may require immediate repayment upon transfer of the property.

Subject-to-financing can be an alternative strategy for buyers and sellers in real estate transactions. It offers the potential for buyers to acquire properties without obtaining new loans, while sellers can benefit from faster sales and financial relief. However, the risks and legal considerations associated with subject-to-financing should not be overlooked. Both parties should thoroughly understand the implications, seek professional advice, and conduct due diligence to ensure a successful transaction. With proper understanding and careful execution, subject-to financing can be a viable option in certain real estate scenarios.

14.5 Lease Options: Renting with the Option to Own

Lease options are a real estate arrangement that provides tenants with the opportunity to rent a property with an option to purchase it at a predetermined price within a specific time frame. This arrangement offers flexibility for both buyers and sellers, allowing tenants to test out the property before committing to a purchase and providing sellers with potential buyers who are already invested in the property. In this section, we will explore lease options, highlighting the advantages and considerations for both buyers and sellers in these agreements.

Understanding Lease Options

In a lease option agreement, the tenant *signs a lease* with the property owner, typically for a specified period, while also obtaining the *option to buy the property* at a predetermined price during the lease term. This option fee, which is usually non-refundable, grants the tenant the *exclusive right to purchase the property* within the agreed-upon timeframe. The lease option provides tenants with the opportunity to experience living in the property before committing to a purchase, while sellers benefit from potential buyers who have a vested interest in the property.

Advantages for Buyers

Lease options offer several advantages for potential buyers.

1. Firstly, it allows buyers to *live in the property and test it out before deciding to purchase*. This provides an opportunity to evaluate the property's condition, neighborhood, and

suitability to their needs.

2. Additionally, lease options give buyers *time to save for a down payment* or *improve their creditworthiness* while securing a future purchase price.
3. If the property's value increases during the lease term, *buyers can benefit from potential appreciation*, allowing them to buy at a lower price than the market value.

Advantages for Sellers

Sellers also stand to benefit from lease options.

1. Firstly, lease options can attract potential buyers who may not qualify for traditional financing at the time but have the intention to purchase in the future. This *expands the pool of potential buyers* and *increases the likelihood of a successful sale.*
2. Sellers can also *earn rental income* during the lease term, making the property financially productive while waiting for the buyer's decision.
3. If the tenant ultimately decides not to exercise the option, the seller *retains the option fee* and can continue to market the property to other potential buyers.

Considerations for Both Parties

Both buyers and sellers must carefully consider certain factors when entering into a lease option agreement. Buyers should ensure they have a *clear understanding of the purchase price, lease term, option fee*, and any *rent credits that may be applicable.* It is crucial to review the terms of the agreement and consult with professionals to avoid potential pitfalls. Sellers, on the other hand, should evaluate the financial stability and credibility of the tenant-buyer to minimize the risk of non-completion of the purchase. Legal advice is essential to draft a comprehensive lease option agreement that protects the interests of both parties.

Lease options offer a flexible and mutually beneficial arrangement for buyers and sellers in the real estate market. Buyers can rent a property while having the option to purchase it at a predetermined price within a specific time frame, allowing them to evaluate the property and secure a future purchase price. Sellers benefit from potential buyers who are already invested in the property and can earn rental income during the lease term. However, it is crucial for both parties to carefully consider the terms, financial implications, and legal aspects of lease options to ensure a successful and satisfactory transaction.

14.6 Identifying Situations Where Creative Financing Can Be Used: Unleashing Opportunities in Real Estate

Creative financing strategies in real estate offer alternative approaches to traditional financing methods, providing opportunities for buyers and sellers to navigate unique situations. In this section, we will explore various scenarios where creative financing can be utilized, enabling individuals to recognize and seize opportunities in real estate transactions. Whether it's overcoming limited financing options, dealing with distressed properties, or seeking mutually beneficial arrangements, creative financing can be a powerful tool in the right circumstances.

Limited Traditional Financing Options

One common situation where creative financing comes into play is when *buyers face challenges obtaining traditional financing*. This could be due to factors such as a low credit score, self-employment status, or insufficient down payment funds. Creative financing techniques, such as seller financing or lease options, can provide viable alternatives for buyers to secure a property without relying on conventional loans. By exploring these options, buyers expand their possibilities and increase their chances of homeownership.

Distressed Property Deals

Distressed properties, such as foreclosures or properties in need of significant repairs, present *unique opportunities for creative financing.* Traditional lenders may be hesitant to finance distressed properties due to their uncertain value or condition. However, investors can leverage creative financing strategies like the BRRRR method or subject-to-financing to acquire and rehabilitate distressed properties. By utilizing these techniques, investors can take advantage of discounted purchase prices, turn the property around, and generate profits.

Seeking Mutually Beneficial Arrangements

Creative financing can also be employed when buyers and sellers are looking for *mutually beneficial arrangements* that traditional financing may not accommodate. For instance, a buyer may be interested in purchasing a property but lacks the necessary down payment. In this case, the buyer and seller can negotiate a rent-to-own agreement, allowing the buyer to rent the property with a portion of the rent going towards a future down payment. This arrangement benefits both parties by providing the buyer with time to save for a down payment and securing a potential buyer for the seller.

Unique Investment Opportunities

Creative financing can be particularly advantageous when presented with unique investment opportunities. For example, a property may have *significant income potential*, but traditional lenders may not recognize or account for that potential in their financing decisions. In such cases, investors can explore creative financing options, such as private loans or joint ventures, to secure funding for the investment. This allows investors to capitalize on opportunities that may not be accessible through conventional financing channels.

Creative financing techniques offer a wide range of possibilities for buyers, sellers, and investors in real estate transactions. By identifying situations where traditional financing options may be limited, dealing with distressed properties, seeking mutually beneficial arrangements, or encountering unique investment opportunities, individuals can leverage creative financing strategies to achieve their goals. It is essential to understand the legal and financial implications of each technique and seek professional advice when necessary. With the right approach and careful consideration, creative financing can unlock new horizons and maximize opportunities in the dynamic real estate market.

14.7 Negotiating Terms for Creative Financing: Structuring Favorable Agreements

Negotiating terms for creative financing is a crucial aspect of real estate transactions. Whether you are a buyer, seller, or investor, understanding how to negotiate and structure favorable terms is essential for successful creative financing arrangements. In this section, we will provide guidance on negotiating key aspects of creative financing, including interest rates, repayment schedules, down payments, and exit strategies. By employing effective negotiation strategies, you can secure terms that align with your goals and maximize the benefits of creative financing.

Interest Rates

Negotiating the interest rate is a critical component of any financing arrangement. In creative financing, the interest rate can vary based on factors such as the buyer's creditworthiness, market conditions, and the risk associated with the transaction. As a buyer, aim to *negotiate a competitive interest rate* that reflects your financial situation and the overall market. Sellers, on the other hand, should consider the prevailing interest rates and the risk they are assuming in the financing arrangement. Conducting research, presenting a strong financial profile, and leveraging alternative financing options can help you negotiate favorable interest rates.

Repayment Schedules

The repayment schedule outlines how the loan will be repaid over time. Negotiating the repayment schedule allows you to align the structure of payments with your financial capabilities and investment goals. As a buyer, consider *negotiating a repayment schedule that accommodates your cash flow* and provides flexibility. For instance, you may negotiate for interest-only payments during an initial period or seek graduated payments that increase over time. Sellers can also propose alternative repayment schedules that meet their needs, such as balloon payments or longer loan terms. Finding a balance that works for both parties is crucial for a successful negotiation.

Down Payments

Negotiating the down payment amount is another important aspect of creative financing. Buyers should aim to negotiate a down payment that aligns with their financial situation and investment objectives. A *larger down payment can help secure more favorable terms*, such as a lower interest rate or reduced loan-to-value ratio. Sellers, on the other hand, may consider offering flexible down payment options to attract potential buyers. Negotiating the down payment amount requires an understanding of your financial capacity and the willingness to explore different possibilities to find a mutually beneficial arrangement.

Exit Strategies

Exit strategies refer to the plans for terminating the creative financing arrangement. Buyers should consider negotiating exit strategies that provide flexibility and options to adjust the financing structure in the future. For example, negotiating an *option to refinance the property* or sell it within a specific timeframe can provide an exit strategy if circumstances change. Sellers should also consider exit strategies that protect their interests, such as *provisions for prepayment penalties* or provisions that allow them to reassess the arrangement if the buyer defaults on payments. Negotiating well-defined exit strategies ensures that both parties have a clear path forward in various scenarios.

Negotiating terms for creative financing is a skill that can significantly impact the success of real estate transactions. By effectively negotiating interest rates, repayment schedules, down payments, and exit strategies, you can structure favorable agreements that align with your objectives. Remember to conduct thorough research, leverage professional advice, and approach negotiations with a clear understanding of your financial capabilities and investment goals. With proper negotiation strategies, you can secure terms that optimize the benefits of creative financing and set the stage for a successful real estate transaction.

14.8 Understanding the Potential Risks and Rewards of Creative Financing: Assessing Outcomes and Managing Risks

Creative financing strategies offer unique opportunities in real estate transactions. While they can provide advantages such as increased access to financing and greater flexibility, it is important to understand the potential risks involved. In this section, we will explore the potential risks and rewards associated with creative financing. By gaining a balanced understanding of the potential outcomes, readers will be equipped to assess the risks and rewards before pursuing creative financing options.

Advantages of Creative Financing

1. *Increased Access to Financing:* Creative financing opens doors for individuals who may have difficulty obtaining traditional financing. It provides alternative options that consider factors beyond credit scores and down payments, allowing more individuals to participate in real estate transactions.
2. *Flexibility in Terms:* Creative financing offers greater flexibility in structuring loan terms. Parties involved can negotiate interest rates, repayment schedules, and down payment amounts to suit their specific needs and circumstances. This flexibility allows for customized arrangements that may not be available through traditional financing methods.
3. *Opportunities for Profit:* Creative financing can present opportunities for profit, particularly for investors. Strategies like house hacking, the BRRRR method, and lease options can generate rental income, appreciation, or potential equity gains. By leveraging these strategies effectively, investors can build wealth and achieve financial goals.

Risks of Creative Financing

1. *Legal and Regulatory Complexities:* Creative financing strategies often involve complex legal and regulatory considerations. Sellers, buyers, and investors must navigate various laws, contracts, and disclosures to ensure compliance and protect their interests. Failing to understand and adhere to legal requirements can result in legal disputes or financial consequences.
2. *Financial Pitfalls:* While creative financing can offer flexibility, it also carries financial risks. Buyers may face higher interest rates, balloon payments, or variable rates that can lead to increased costs over time. Investors taking on distressed properties may encounter *unforeseen repair and maintenance expenses*. It is crucial to conduct thorough financial analysis and consider potential risks before committing to a creative financing arrangement.
3. *Market Volatility and Uncertainty:* Real estate markets are subject to volatility and fluctuations. Economic downturns, changes in interest rates, and local market conditions can impact the value and profitability of properties involved in creative financing arrangements. Assessing market trends and potential risks is essential to make informed decisions and mitigate the impact of market uncertainties.
4. *Dependence on Counterparty:* Creative financing often relies on the cooperation and trust of the counterparty. Sellers acting as lenders, for example, may require ongoing communication and collaboration with buyers. The success of the arrangement can be influenced by the financial stability, integrity, and reliability of the counterparty involved.

Before pursuing creative financing options, it is crucial to assess the risks and rewards associated with each strategy. Conducting thorough due diligence, consulting professionals, and analyzing financial projections can help evaluate potential outcomes. Consider factors such as property value, financial stability, market conditions, and legal implications. It is essential to have a realistic understanding of the potential risks and rewards and make informed decisions that align with your financial goals and risk tolerance.

Conclusion

Creative financing strategies in real estate, such as house hacking, the BRRRR method, seller financing, subject-to-financing, and lease options, offer unique opportunities for individuals to generate income, access financing, and create mutually beneficial arrangements. However, it is crucial to understand the risks involved and conduct thorough due diligence. By approaching creative financing with informed decision-making, negotiating favorable terms, and assessing risks and rewards, individuals can leverage these strategies to achieve their real estate goals. With a comprehensive understanding and careful consideration, creative financing can open up new possibilities and facilitate successful transactions.

Chapter 15: Real Estate Financing Risks and Challenges

Risky - Photo by geralt

15.1 Interest Rate Fluctuations: Managing Risk in Real Estate Financing

Interest rates play a significant role in real estate financing, and fluctuations in these rates can have a profound impact on borrowing costs, mortgage payments, and overall profitability. In this section, we will explore the risks associated with interest rate fluctuations and discuss strategies for managing interest rate risk in real estate financing. By understanding the factors that influence interest rates and implementing appropriate risk management strategies, readers will be better equipped to navigate the dynamic landscape of interest rate fluctuations.

Factors Influencing Interest Rates

Before delving into the risks and strategies, it is essential to understand the factors that influence interest rates. Interest rates are influenced by a variety of factors, including:

1. *Economic Conditions:* The overall state of the economy, including inflation, GDP growth, employment rates, and monetary policies set by central banks, can impact interest rates. When the economy is strong, interest rates tend to rise to curb inflation, whereas during economic downturns, central banks may lower interest rates to stimulate economic activity.
2. *Federal Reserve Policies:* The monetary policies implemented by the Federal Reserve, such as adjusting the federal funds rate, can have a direct impact on interest rates. Changes in the federal funds rate ripple through the financial system, affecting borrowing costs for mortgages and other loans.
3. *Supply and Demand for Credit:* The supply and demand dynamics in the credit market also influence interest rates. When there is high demand for credit, interest rates tend to rise. Conversely, when credit demand is low, interest rates may decrease.

Managing Interest Rate Risk

Given the potential impact of interest rate fluctuations on real estate financing, it is important to employ strategies to manage interest rate risk. Here are some approaches to consider:

1. *Fixed-Rate Mortgages:* Opting for a fixed-rate mortgage locks in an interest rate for the duration of the loan. This provides

stability and protects borrowers from future interest rate increases. Even if interest rates rise, the mortgage payment remains constant, offering predictability and budgeting ease.

2. *Adjustable-Rate Mortgages (ARMs):* ARMs have interest rates that adjust periodically based on predetermined factors, such as the movement of a benchmark rate. While ARMs typically offer lower initial interest rates, they can increase over time. Borrowers should carefully assess their ability to handle potential rate adjustments and consider factors such as rate caps and adjustment periods.
3. *Rate Locks:* When obtaining financing, borrowers can request a rate lock from the lender. A rate lock guarantees a specific interest rate for a defined period, protecting the borrower from subsequent rate increases. However, rate locks may come with associated fees, and borrowers should carefully evaluate the duration of the lock and the terms of the agreement.
4. *Diversification of Financing:* Investors with multiple properties or a real estate portfolio can diversify their financing options. By using a mix of fixed-rate and adjustable-rate mortgages, they can mitigate the impact of interest rate fluctuations. This approach spreads the risk and provides flexibility based on the individual properties and investment goals.
5. *Refinancing:* Refinancing allows borrowers to replace their existing mortgage with a new loan at a different interest rate. When interest rates decline, refinancing to obtain a lower rate can reduce borrowing costs and monthly payments. However, refinancing comes with associated costs, such as closing fees, and borrowers should consider the breakeven point and potential savings before proceeding.
6. *Monitoring Market Conditions:* Staying informed about

market conditions and interest rate trends is crucial in managing interest rate risk. Keeping an eye on economic indicators, central bank policies, and forecasts can help borrowers anticipate potential rate changes and make informed decisions regarding their financing.

In summary, managing interest rate fluctuations in real estate financing is essential for financial stability and profitability. Implementing strategies such as fixed-rate mortgages, appropriate risk assessment for adjustable-rate mortgages, rate locks, diversification of financing, refinancing opportunities, and staying informed about market conditions can mitigate the impact of interest rate changes. It is crucial to tailor these strategies to individual circumstances and consult with professionals for guidance. Thorough financial analysis, stress testing, sensitivity analysis, and scenario planning are necessary to assess the potential risks and make informed decisions. By proactively managing interest rate risk, borrowers can protect their investments and achieve long-term success in real estate financing.

15.2 Market Volatility: Navigating Challenges in Real Estate Financing

Market volatility is an inherent characteristic of the real estate industry. Economic downturns, changes in property values, and fluctuations in demand and supply can significantly impact real estate financing. In this section, we will explore the challenges posed by market volatility and discuss strategies for navigating these challenges. By understanding the potential impact of market volatility and implementing appropriate risk management strategies, readers will be better equipped to navigate the dynamic real estate landscape.

Impact of Economic Downturns

During economic downturns, the real estate market often experiences reduced demand, declining property values, and tighter credit conditions. This can pose challenges for real estate financing, including:

1. *Decreased Property Values:* Economic downturns can lead to a decline in property values, potentially affecting the appraised value of collateral for financing. This can result in lower loan-to-value ratios and impact borrowing capacity.
2. *Reduced Financing Options:* Lenders may tighten their lending standards during economic downturns, making it more difficult for borrowers to secure financing. Lenders may require higher credit scores, larger down payments, and stricter income verification, resulting in limited financing options.
3. *Cash Flow Challenges:* Economic downturns can impact rental income, occupancy rates, and cash flow from investment properties. This can affect borrowers' ability to meet mortgage payments, potentially leading to financial strain and increased default risk.

Strategies for Navigating Market Volatility

While market volatility poses challenges, there are strategies that borrowers can employ to navigate these uncertainties:

1. *Building Reserves:* Establishing a financial cushion through cash reserves can help borrowers weather market downturns. Maintaining adequate reserves can provide a buffer during periods of reduced cash flow, allowing borrowers to continue

meeting their financial obligations.

2. *Stress Testing and Scenario Analysis:* Conducting stress tests and scenario analysis can help borrowers evaluate the potential impact of market volatility on their real estate investments. By modeling different market conditions, borrowers can assess their ability to withstand adverse scenarios and make informed decisions.
3. *Diversification:* Diversifying real estate investments across different locations, property types, and markets can help mitigate the impact of market volatility. A well-diversified portfolio can provide stability and potentially offset losses in one area with gains in another.
4. *Long-Term Investment Perspective:* Real estate is typically a long-term investment. By adopting a long-term perspective, borrowers can ride out short-term market fluctuations and benefit from the potential appreciation and income generation over the investment horizon.
5. *Monitoring Market Trends:* Staying informed about market trends, economic indicators, and forecasts is crucial in navigating market volatility. By monitoring the real estate market and economic conditions, borrowers can make informed decisions regarding property acquisitions, refinancing opportunities, and risk management strategies.
6. *Collaboration with Professionals:* Seeking guidance from real estate professionals, financial advisors, and mortgage experts can provide valuable insights and guidance in navigating market volatility. These professionals can provide expertise, market knowledge, and help identify appropriate strategies to mitigate risks and optimize real estate financing.

Market volatility poses challenges in real estate financing. By understanding the potential impact of economic downturns, changes in property values, and fluctuations in demand and supply, borrowers can implement effective strategies to navigate these challenges. Building reserves, stress testing, diversification, maintaining a long-term perspective, monitoring market trends, and collaborating with professionals are important approaches to managing market volatility. By proactively managing risks and adapting to changing market conditions, borrowers can navigate market volatility and position themselves for success in real estate financing.

15.3 Financing Fees and Costs: Understanding the Financial Implications in Real Estate Financing

Real estate financing involves various fees and costs that borrowers need to consider. These expenses can significantly impact the overall profitability of an investment property or the affordability of a residential property. In this section, we will explore the different fees and costs associated with real estate financing. By understanding these financial implications, readers will be better equipped to plan their budgets, evaluate the affordability of financing options, and make informed decisions.

Loan Origination Fees

Loan origination fees are charges levied by lenders for processing a loan application. These fees typically cover administrative costs, credit checks, underwriting, and other services provided by the lender. Loan origination fees are usually a percentage of the loan amount and can range from 0.5% to 1% or more. It is important for borrowers to factor in these fees when assessing the total cost of borrowing.

Closing Costs

Closing costs encompass a variety of expenses incurred during the closing process of a real estate transaction. These costs can include:

1. *Appraisal Fees:* Lenders often require an appraisal to determine the market value of the property. Appraisal fees vary depending on the property's size, location, and complexity. It is important to budget for this expense, as it is typically paid upfront.
2. *Title Insurance:* Title insurance protects lenders and buyers from potential defects in the property's title. The cost of title insurance can vary depending on the property's value and location. It is a one-time fee paid at closing.
3. *Attorney or Escrow Fees:* Engaging an attorney or escrow company is common during real estate transactions. These professionals ensure that the closing process is legally sound and facilitate the transfer of funds and ownership. Their fees can vary based on the complexity of the transaction.
4. *Recording Fees:* Recording fees are charges imposed by the government for recording the property transaction documents in public records. The fees can vary depending on the location and the number of documents being recorded.

Ongoing Maintenance Costs

Beyond the upfront fees and costs, borrowers must also consider ongoing maintenance costs associated with the property. These expenses can include:

1. *Property Taxes:* Property taxes are levied by local governments and can vary based on the property's assessed

value and the local tax rates. It is important to account for property taxes when evaluating the affordability of real estate financing.

2. *Insurance Premiums:* Property insurance is necessary to protect against risks such as fire, theft, and natural disasters. Insurance premiums can vary based on the property type, location, and coverage levels.
3. *Homeowners Association (HOA) Fees:* In certain communities, homeowners may be required to pay HOA fees for shared amenities, maintenance, and other services. HOA fees can vary widely and should be considered when evaluating the affordability of a property.

Understanding the various fees and costs associated with real estate financing is crucial for borrowers. Loan origination fees, closing costs, appraisal fees, and ongoing maintenance costs can significantly impact the overall financial picture of a real estate investment or residential property purchase. By factoring in these expenses when evaluating financing options and budgeting for property ownership, borrowers can make informed decisions, assess the affordability of the investment, and ensure long-term financial stability. It is advisable for borrowers to work closely with lenders, real estate professionals, and financial advisors to gain a comprehensive understanding of the fees and costs involved and make sound financial decisions in their real estate financing endeavors.

15.4 Defaulting on Your Loan: Understanding the Risks and Mitigation Strategies

Defaulting on a real estate loan can have significant consequences for borrowers. It is crucial to understand the risks associated with loan default and implement effective strategies to mitigate those risks. In this section, we will examine the consequences of loan default, the importance of assessing financial capabilities, maintaining proper cash reserves, and implementing risk management strategies to avoid default.

Consequences of Loan Default

1. *Foreclosure:* One of the primary consequences of loan default is the possibility of foreclosure. When borrowers default on their loan payments, lenders have the right to initiate foreclosure proceedings, leading to the seizure and sale of the property to recover the outstanding debt. Foreclosure can result in the loss of the property and any equity accumulated.
2. *Damage to Creditworthiness:* Loan default can have a significant negative impact on a borrower's creditworthiness. The late payments, delinquencies, and foreclosure associated with default are reported to credit bureaus and can result in a lowered credit score. This can make it challenging to obtain future loans and may lead to higher interest rates or unfavorable loan terms.

Assessing Financial Capabilities

To avoid defaulting on a loan, borrowers should assess their financial capabilities before entering into a loan agreement. This involves:

1. *Evaluating Income and Expenses:* Determining whether the income generated from the property or personal income is sufficient to cover loan payments, property expenses, and other financial obligations.
2. *Calculating Debt-to-Income Ratio:* Assessing the debt-to-income ratio, which compares monthly debt payments to monthly income. Lenders typically have maximum debt-to-

income ratios that borrowers must adhere to.

3. *Considering Future Financial Scenarios:* Anticipating potential changes in income, such as job loss or increased expenses, and assessing whether the borrower's financial situation can withstand those changes.

Maintaining Proper Cash Reserves

Maintaining adequate cash reserves is crucial in avoiding loan default. Cash reserves provide a financial buffer during unexpected events or periods of financial hardship. Here are some considerations:

1. *Establishing an Emergency Fund:* Building an emergency fund that can cover several months' worth of loan payments and property expenses can help borrowers navigate unforeseen circumstances.
2. *Planning for Property Maintenance:* Budgeting for ongoing property maintenance and repairs can prevent financial strain and ensure that unexpected expenses do not lead to loan default.

Implementing Risk Management Strategies

To mitigate the risk of loan default, borrowers should implement effective risk management strategies:

1. *Budgeting and Financial Planning:* Creating a comprehensive budget and financial plan can help borrowers track income and expenses, allocate funds for loan payments, and ensure that sufficient cash reserves are maintained.
2. *Exploring Loan Modification Options:* In the event of financial hardship, borrowers can consider loan modification

options, such as refinancing or adjusting loan terms, to make payments more manageable.

3. *Communication with Lenders:* Open and proactive communication with lenders is crucial. If borrowers anticipate difficulty in making loan payments, contacting the lender early on can help explore potential solutions and avoid default.

Defaulting on a real estate loan can have severe consequences, including foreclosure and damage to creditworthiness. By assessing their financial capabilities, maintaining proper cash reserves, and implementing risk management strategies, borrowers can mitigate the risk of loan default. Evaluating income and expenses, calculating debt-to-income ratios, and considering future financial scenarios are essential in assessing financial capabilities. Furthermore, establishing emergency funds, planning for property maintenance, and exploring loan modification options can help borrowers navigate financial challenges. Effective communication with lenders is key to addressing financial difficulties and finding potential solutions.

15.5 Managing Risk and Mitigating Challenges: Proactive Strategies in Real Estate Financing

Real estate financing involves various risks and challenges that borrowers need to address to ensure successful outcomes. By implementing proactive risk management strategies and mitigating potential challenges, borrowers can enhance their financial stability and protect their investments. In this section, we will explore strategies for managing risk and mitigating challenges in real estate financing.

Diversify Investments

Diversification is a fundamental risk management strategy that applies to real estate financing as well. By diversifying their investment portfolio across different property types, locations, and financing options, borrowers can reduce their exposure to specific risks. Diversification allows for a more balanced and resilient investment strategy, as any negative impact on one property or market segment may be offset by the performance of other investments.

Conduct Thorough Due Diligence

Thorough due diligence is crucial in real estate financing. This involves conducting comprehensive research and analysis of potential properties, lenders, and financing options. Key elements of due diligence include:

- *Property Evaluation:* Assessing the property's condition, market value, rental potential, and potential risks such as environmental issues or legal restrictions.
- *Lender Evaluation:* Reviewing the reputation, track record, and terms of potential lenders to ensure they align with the borrower's financial goals and risk tolerance.
- *Financing Options:* Evaluating the terms, interest rates, fees, and potential risks associated with different financing options to make an informed decision.

By conducting thorough due diligence, borrowers can identify and mitigate potential risks before committing to a financing arrangement.

Maintain Financial Reserves

Maintaining adequate financial reserves is essential for managing unforeseen challenges or emergencies. Financial reserves can help cover unexpected expenses, such as repairs, vacancies, or economic downturns. By setting aside a portion of rental income or profits from real estate investments, borrowers can establish a safety net to protect against financial instability.

Obtain Appropriate Insurance Coverage

Insurance plays a critical role in risk management for real estate financing. It is crucial to obtain appropriate insurance coverage to protect against potential liabilities and losses. Some common insurance types include:

- *Property Insurance:* Protects against damages to the property caused by natural disasters, fire, theft, or vandalism.
- *Liability Insurance:* Provides coverage in the event of accidents or injuries that occur on the property.
- *Rent Loss Insurance:* Offers protection against income loss due to tenant default or property damage.

By obtaining comprehensive insurance coverage, borrowers can mitigate potential financial losses and protect their investment properties.

Stay Informed about Market Trends

Staying informed about market trends and developments is essential for proactive risk management in real estate financing. By monitoring market conditions, economic indicators, and regulatory changes, borrowers can anticipate potential challenges and adjust their strategies accordingly. Regularly reviewing market trends enables borrowers to make informed decisions about financing, property acquisitions, and investment strategies.

Managing risk and mitigating challenges in real estate financing requires proactive strategies and diligent decision-making. Diversifying investments, conducting thorough due diligence, maintaining financial reserves, obtaining appropriate insurance coverage, and staying informed about market trends are key elements of a comprehensive risk management approach. By implementing these strategies, borrowers can enhance their financial stability, protect their investments, and navigate potential challenges effectively. It is important for borrowers to continuously assess their risk exposure, adapt their strategies to changing market conditions, and seek professional advice when needed.

Conclusion

In conclusion, real estate financing is a complex process that requires careful consideration and proactive risk management. By understanding and navigating the risks associated with interest rate fluctuations, market volatility, financing fees and costs, and loan default, borrowers can increase their chances of successful outcomes. It is crucial to stay informed about market trends, conduct thorough due diligence, and negotiate favorable terms. Additionally, borrowers should assess their financial capabilities, maintain cash reserves, and implement risk management strategies to protect their investments. By taking these steps, borrowers can navigate the challenges of real estate financing and position themselves for long-term success in the real estate market.

Chapter 16: Refinancing Your Mortgage

Mortgage - Photo by mohamed_hassan

16.1 Introduction to Mortgage Refinancing:

Mortgage refinancing is a process that entails obtaining a new loan to replace an existing mortgage. Property owners opt for mortgage refinancing for a variety of reasons, driven by their financial goals and changing circumstances. One primary purpose of mortgage refinancing is to **secure more favorable terms** that can lead to cost savings over the life of the loan. By refinancing, property owners can potentially take advantage of lower interest rates available in the market, especially if rates have decreased since they first obtained their mortgage. A lower interest rate can significantly reduce monthly mortgage payments, freeing up funds for other expenses or allowing property owners to save more.

Another purpose of mortgage refinancing is to **access the equity built in the property**. Over time, as property owners make mortgage payments and property values appreciate, they accumulate equity.

Refinancing provides an opportunity to tap into this equity and convert it into cash. This can be particularly useful for financing home improvements, consolidating high-interest debts, funding education expenses, or pursuing other financial goals.

When considering mortgage refinancing, it's important for property owners to carefully evaluate the **benefits and considerations** associated with the decision. The benefits of refinancing can include not only cost savings through *lower interest rates* but also *increased cash flow* by reducing monthly payments. By refinancing to a lower interest rate or extending the loan term, property owners can potentially reduce their monthly mortgage obligations, which can improve their overall financial situation.

However, there are considerations that property owners need to keep in mind as well. Refinancing often involves **closing costs**, which can include *application fees*, *appraisal fees*, *title search fees*, and *other expenses.* These costs should be weighed against the potential savings and benefits of refinancing to determine if it makes financial sense. Additionally, property owners should consider their long-term plans for the property. If they plan to sell or move in the near future, the potential savings from refinancing may not outweigh the costs.

Several factors can impact the decision and feasibility of mortgage refinancing. Lenders typically consider factors such as *credit score*, *loan-to-value ratio*, *income stability*, and *home equity* when evaluating a borrower's eligibility and determining the terms of refinancing. A higher credit score can lead to more favorable refinancing options, while a lower loan-to-value ratio and increased home equity can result in better interest rates and loan terms. Income stability is important in demonstrating the borrower's ability to make mortgage payments.

In summary, mortgage refinancing provides homeowners with the opportunity to obtain more favorable loan terms, lower monthly payments, and access the equity in their homes. The decision to refinance should consider the benefits, such as potential cost savings and improved cash flow, as well as the considerations, including closing costs and long-term plans for the property. Factors such as credit score, loan-to-value ratio, income stability, and equity impact eligibility for refinancing. Timing is also crucial, taking into account current interest rates, personal circumstances, and financial goals.

16.2 How Mortgage Refinancing Works

Mortgage refinancing is a process that involves replacing your current mortgage with a new one, usually to obtain more favorable terms or achieve specific financial goals. Understanding how mortgage refinancing works is crucial for property owners looking to make informed decisions about their mortgage options. This section will provide a comprehensive overview of the steps involved in the mortgage refinancing process.

Determining Eligibility for Refinancing

Before beginning the refinancing process, property owners must first determine if they are eligible. Factors that can impact eligibility include *credit score*, *debt-to-income ratio*, *employment status*, and the *current value of the property*. Lenders may also consider factors such as payment history, equity in the property, and the purpose of the refinance.

Gathering Documentation

Once eligibility has been established, property owners will need to gather relevant documentation for the refinancing application process. This typically includes income and employment verification, tax returns, bank statements, and documentation related to any outstanding debts. It is important to have all documentation ready before beginning the application process to avoid delays or complications.

Choosing a Lender

When choosing a lender, property owners should consider factors such as interest rates, loan terms, fees, and reputation. It is important to shop around and compare offers from multiple lenders to ensure that the best terms and conditions are obtained. Additionally, property owners may want to consider working with a lender that has experience with mortgage refinancing specifically.

Application and Approval Process

Once a lender has been chosen, property owners will need to complete the refinancing application process. This typically involves filling out an application, submitting relevant documentation, and undergoing a credit check. The lender will then review the application and determine if the property owner meets their eligibility requirements. If approved, the property owner will need to sign the loan documents and go through a closing process, which may involve paying closing costs and obtaining title insurance. After closing, the new loan will replace the existing mortgage, and the property owner will begin making payments under the new terms and conditions.

Overall, the refinancing process can be complex and involve significant paperwork and documentation. It is important for property owners to understand the steps involved and work with a reputable lender to ensure a successful refinancing outcome.

16.3 Pros and Cons of Mortgage Refinancing

Mortgage refinancing can offer several benefits, but it's important to weigh them against potential drawbacks. In this section, we will provide an objective analysis of the pros and cons of mortgage refinancing to help readers make an informed decision.

Pros of Mortgage Refinancing

1. *Lower Interest Rates:* One of the primary reasons property owners consider refinancing is to secure a lower interest rate. By refinancing at a lower rate, property owners can potentially save thousands of dollars in interest payments over the life of the loan.
2. *Reduced Monthly Payments:* Refinancing can also lead to lower monthly mortgage payments. This can free up additional cash flow, providing property owners with more financial flexibility and the ability to allocate funds to other priorities.
3. *Access to Equity:* Refinancing allows property owners to tap into their equity by borrowing against it. This can be particularly beneficial for funding improvements, paying off high-interest debts, or covering major expenses such as education or medical bills.
4. *Consolidation of Debt:* Property owners who have accumulated multiple high-interest debts can use mortgage refinancing to consolidate their debts into a single, more manageable payment. This can simplify financial management and potentially save money by securing a lower interest rate.

Cons of Mortgage Refinancing

1. *Extended Loan Terms:* Refinancing often resets the loan term, which means property owners may end up with a longer repayment period. While this can result in lower monthly payments, it also means paying interest over a longer period, potentially increasing the overall cost of the loan.
2. *Closing Costs:* Refinancing typically involves upfront costs, such as loan origination fees, appraisal fees, title search fees, and closing costs. These expenses can add up and may take several years to recoup through the savings generated by the refinanced loan.
3. *Potential Impact on Credit Scores:* Refinancing requires a credit check, and multiple credit inquiries within a short period can temporarily lower credit scores. Additionally, if property owners fail to make timely payments on the new loan, it can negatively affect their creditworthiness.
4. *Risk of Overborrowing:* Refinancing can tempt property owners to access the equity in their property without careful consideration. Borrowing against their equity should be done responsibly, taking into account the long-term financial implications and the potential risk of being "house poor."

It is essential for property owners to carefully evaluate the potential benefits and drawbacks of refinancing and assess how it aligns with their long-term financial goals. Consulting with a financial advisor or mortgage professional can provide valuable guidance in making an informed decision.

Conclusion

In conclusion, mortgage refinancing offers property owners the opportunity to achieve their financial goals and overcome specific challenges. By understanding the process, carefully considering the reasons for refinancing, and weighing the pros and cons, property owners can make informed decisions that align with their unique circumstances. Seeking professional advice and guidance is crucial to ensure that refinancing is the right choice for individual needs. property owners should also be aware of the potential costs involved and how they may impact their overall financial situation. By approaching mortgage refinancing with diligence and a comprehensive understanding, property owners can leverage this tool effectively to improve their financial well-being and achieve their long-term objectives.

Chapter 17: Summary: Real Estate Financing and Investment Goals

Realistic Goals - Photo by Fernanda Greppe

17.1 Setting Your Investment Goals

Setting clear investment goals is a crucial step in real estate financing. Without well-defined objectives, investors may find themselves adrift in the vast sea of opportunities, lacking a sense of direction and purpose. In this section, we emphasize the significance of setting specific, measurable, achievable, relevant, and time-bound (SMART) goals to guide real estate investment decisions.

Defining Your Objectives

Defining your objectives is a critical step in real estate financing. By reflecting on your *personal and financial aspirations*, you can determine what you hope to achieve through your real estate investments. Whether it's generating *passive income*, building *long-term wealth*, *diversifying your investment portfolio*, or *reaching specific financial milestones*, clarifying these objectives is essential. This process allows you to set a clear direction and purpose for your investment journey, guiding your decisions and actions moving forward.

Creating SMART Goals

The concept of SMART goals provides a valuable framework for setting objectives that are **S**pecific, **M**easurable, **A**chievable, **R**elevant, and **T**ime-bound. Instead of vague or generalized goals, SMART goals are well-defined and actionable. By transforming your broad investment objectives into specific targets, you bring *clarity and focus to your investment decisions*. For instance, rather than aiming to "build wealth," a SMART goal could be *"to acquire five rental properties with a net annual cash flow of $50,000 within the next five years"*. SMART goals enable effective progress tracking and evaluation, ensuring that your efforts are directed towards achievable outcomes.

Aligning Goals with Risk Tolerance and Time Horizon

Aligning your goals with your risk tolerance and time horizon is crucial for a suitable investment strategy. Understanding your *comfort level with risk* and the timeframe in which you plan to invest helps you make informed decisions. Investors with a higher risk tolerance and longer time horizon may be inclined to pursue higher-growth opportunities, while those with a lower risk tolerance and shorter time horizon may prioritize stable income-generating properties. By aligning your goals with these factors, you ensure that your investment strategy matches your individual circumstances and preferences, setting you on a path towards success.

Revisiting and Adjusting Goals

Regularly reviewing and adjusting your investment goals is essential as *personal circumstances*, *market conditions*, and *financial landscapes* change over time. By periodically reassessing your goals, you can adapt to new opportunities and challenges. This process involves *evaluating your progress*, *identifying areas for improvement*, and *making necessary adjustments* to stay on track. By revisiting and adjusting your goals, you ensure their ongoing relevance and effectiveness, enabling you to navigate the dynamic nature of your financial journey successfully.

Taking Action

Taking action based on your defined goals is crucial for progress and success. Creating a plan and implementing strategies that align with your objectives is key to moving closer to your investment goals. This may involve developing a comprehensive investment plan, conducting market research, building a network of professionals, and executing real estate financing transactions effectively. By *actively pursuing your goals* and utilizing the guidance and resources available, you can confidently progress on your investment journey and work towards achieving your desired outcomes.

In summary, setting clear investment goals is a fundamental step in real estate financing. Defining your objectives allows you to establish a sense of purpose and direction in your investment journey. By creating SMART goals that are specific, measurable, achievable, relevant, and time-bound, you bring clarity and focus to your investment decisions. Aligning your goals with your risk tolerance and time horizon ensures that your investment strategy suits your individual circumstances and preferences. Regularly revisiting and adjusting your goals allows you to adapt to changing conditions and seize new opportunities. However, taking action is paramount to making progress and achieving success.

17.2 Planning Your Investment Strategy

Planning an effective investment strategy is essential when venturing into the world of real estate financing. In this section, we will delve into the process of developing a strategic approach that aligns with your investment goals in the real estate market. By understanding different investment strategies, analyzing market conditions, identifying target markets, and aligning your strategy with your goals, you can increase the likelihood of success and make informed decisions throughout your real estate investment journey.

Understanding Investment Strategies

To embark on a successful real estate investment journey, it is crucial to have a solid understanding of various investment strategies. These strategies can include *buy and hold*, *fix and flip*, *commercial properties*, *real estate investment trusts (REITs)*, and more. Each strategy comes with its advantages, risk profiles, and considerations. By familiarizing yourself with these strategies, you can evaluate which one aligns best with your financial goals, risk tolerance, and investment timeline.

Analyzing Market Conditions

Analyzing market conditions is a critical step in developing a real estate investment strategy. It involves researching and assessing factors such as *supply and demand dynamics*, *local economic indicators*, *population growth*, *rental market trends*, and *property valuations*. Understanding market conditions allows you to identify potential opportunities, determine the feasibility of your investment strategy, and mitigate risks. By staying informed about the macro and microeconomic factors impacting the real estate market, you can make strategic decisions that maximize your chances of success.

Identifying Target Markets

Identifying target markets is a key aspect of developing a real estate investment strategy. This involves evaluating *different geographic locations* and narrowing down to markets that offer the most potential for growth, rental income, or value appreciation. Factors to consider when selecting target markets include population trends, job market stability, infrastructure development, and local regulations. By conducting thorough market research and due diligence, you can identify target markets that align with your investment strategy and have the potential for long-term profitability.

Aligning Strategy with Goals

To ensure the effectiveness of your real estate investment strategy, it is crucial to align it with your specific goals and objectives. Are you seeking *cash flow* through rental income, *long-term appreciation*, or a combination of both? Defining your goals helps determine the appropriate investment strategy, property types, and financing options. Additionally, consider your risk tolerance, investment timeline, and personal circumstances when aligning your strategy with your goals. This alignment ensures that your investment approach remains consistent and focused on achieving your desired outcomes.

Executing the Investment Strategy

Executing the investment strategy involves taking concrete steps to *acquire*, *manage,* and *monitor* your real estate investments. This may include activities such as property acquisition, financing, property management, tenant screening, and ongoing evaluation of portfolio performance. Implementing your strategy requires a thorough understanding of the investment process, legal considerations, financing options, and risk management. *Regularly reviewing and adjusting your strategy* based on market conditions and performance indicators is essential to optimize your real estate investments and maximize returns.

In summary, developing an effective real estate investment strategy involves understanding different investment strategies, analyzing market conditions, identifying target markets, aligning your strategy with your goals, and executing the strategy diligently. By considering these key elements, you can make informed decisions and increase the likelihood of success in the dynamic and rewarding realm of real estate financing. Remember to conduct thorough research, stay updated on market trends, and adapt your strategy as needed to navigate the ever-changing landscape of real estate investment.

17.3 Evaluating Your Risk Tolerance

Evaluating your risk tolerance is an essential aspect of real estate financing and investments. Understanding your risk tolerance is crucial because it directly impacts the decisions you make regarding investment opportunities, asset allocation, and overall portfolio management. In this section, we will explore the significance of comprehending your risk tolerance and provide guidance on evaluating and determining your own level of risk tolerance.

Defining Risk Tolerance

Risk tolerance refers to an *individual's willingness and ability to take on risks* in pursuit of investment returns. It is a personal characteristic that varies from person to person and is influenced by factors such as *financial goals*, *time horizon*, and *psychological factors*. Some investors are more comfortable with higher risks and potential volatility, while others prefer lower-risk investments with more stable returns.

Understanding your risk tolerance is crucial in making informed investment decisions that align with your financial objectives.

Assessing Personal Risk Tolerance

Assessing your personal risk tolerance involves considering various factors and understanding your emotional response to risk. It requires self-reflection and evaluation of your *financial goals*, *investment horizon*, *income stability*, and *psychological comfort* with uncertainty. Additionally, considering *past experiences* and how you reacted to market fluctuations can provide valuable insights into your risk tolerance. By honestly assessing your risk tolerance, you can establish a solid foundation for your investment strategy and avoid making decisions that are outside your comfort zone.

Aligning Risk Tolerance with Investment Decisions

Once you have evaluated your risk tolerance, it is important to align it with your investment decisions. This means *selecting investment opportunities and asset classes that are in line with your risk tolerance level.* For example, if you have a conservative risk tolerance, you may opt for more stable investments such as income-generating properties or real estate investment trusts (REITs). On the other hand, if you have a higher risk tolerance, you may be more inclined to invest in high-growth potential properties or take on leverage. Aligning your risk tolerance with your investment decisions helps maintain a balanced and well-suited portfolio.

Managing Risk

Managing risk is a crucial aspect of real estate financing and investments. Diversification, proper due diligence, and thorough research are important risk management techniques. By *diversifying your real estate portfolio across different types of properties, locations, and investment strategies*, you can mitigate the impact of potential risks. Conducting comprehensive due diligence and research on properties, market conditions, and economic indicators can help identify potential risks and opportunities. Regular monitoring and evaluation of your portfolio's performance is also essential to adjust your risk management strategy as needed.

Seeking Professional Advice

If you are unsure about evaluating your risk tolerance or making investment decisions, seeking professional advice from a *financial advisor* or *real estate expert* can provide valuable guidance. These professionals can assess your risk tolerance, help you understand the potential risks and rewards associated with different investment options, and provide recommendations based on your unique circumstances and goals. Their expertise can add an extra layer of confidence and help you navigate the complexities of real estate financing.

In conclusion, evaluating your risk tolerance is a vital step in real estate financing and investments. By understanding and assessing your risk tolerance, aligning it with your investment decisions, managing risk effectively, and seeking professional advice when needed, you can make informed choices that are in line with your financial goals and personal comfort level. Remember that risk tolerance can evolve over time, so regular reassessment is important to ensure your investment strategy remains aligned with your risk profile.

17.4 Identifying Investment Opportunities

Identifying investment opportunities is a vital aspect of real estate financing and investments. It involves thorough market research, property analysis, and exploring various sources to find potential opportunities that align with your goals and investment strategy. In this section, we will provide guidance on how to effectively identify real estate investment opportunities and increase your chances of success in the market.

Conducting Market Research

Conducting comprehensive market research is essential when identifying real estate investment opportunities. This involves analyzing *local market conditions, economic indicators, population trends, job market stability*, and *infrastructure development*. Understanding the supply and demand dynamics of the real estate market can help identify areas with *potential for growth, rental income*, or *value appreciation*. Additionally, staying updated on current and future market trends allows you to make informed decisions and seize opportunities as they arise.

Analyzing Property Trends

Analyzing property trends is a crucial step in identifying investment opportunities. This includes studying factors such as *property prices, rental rates, vacancy rates*, and *property appreciation trends*. By analyzing historical data and current market conditions, you can identify properties that have the potential for positive cash flow, strong appreciation, or other desirable investment characteristics. Additionally, considering factors such as property types, neighborhoods, and amenities can help narrow down potential opportunities that align with your investment strategy.

Identifying Emerging or Undervalued Markets

Identifying emerging or undervalued markets can provide unique investment opportunities. These markets may offer the potential for growth and value appreciation before they become mainstream. By staying informed about *economic development plans*, *urban revitalization initiatives*, or *demographic shifts*, you can identify markets that are poised for growth. Investing in emerging or undervalued markets requires thorough research and due diligence to assess the risks and potential rewards associated with these opportunities.

Sources for Finding Investment Opportunities

There are various sources for finding real estate investment opportunities. These include *online listings platforms*, *real estate agents*, *networking with other investors*, attending *property auctions*, and exploring *off-market deals*.

1. *Online platforms* and *real estate agents* provide access to a wide range of properties for sale,
2. *networking with other investors* can uncover off-market opportunities or joint venture possibilities,
3. *property auctions* can be a source of distressed properties or investment deals, but they require careful evaluation and due diligence.

Exploring different sources can increase your chances of finding suitable investment opportunities.

In conclusion, identifying investment opportunities in real estate financing and investments requires conducting market research, analyzing property trends, identifying emerging or undervalued markets, and exploring various sources for potential deals. Thorough research and analysis are crucial in assessing the viability and potential risks of investment opportunities. By staying informed, being proactive in your search, and leveraging different sources, you can increase your chances of finding real estate investment opportunities that align with your goals and investment strategy. Remember to exercise due diligence and consult professionals when needed to make well-informed investment decisions.

17.5 Final: Creating a Long-term Investment Plan

Creating a long-term investment plan is crucial for achieving success in real estate financing. It involves developing a comprehensive and strategic approach that aligns with your long-term goals and aspirations. In this section, we will provide guidance on building a diversified portfolio, setting investment milestones, leveraging financing options, and managing cash flow to ensure a robust and sustainable investment plan.

Building a Diversified Portfolio

Building a diversified portfolio is a key component of a long-term investment plan. Diversification involves *spreading your investments across different types of properties, locations, and investment strategies*. This helps mitigate risks by reducing exposure to any single asset or market. Consider investing in a mix of residential, commercial, and rental properties, as well as diversifying across various geographic areas. Additionally, exploring different investment strategies, such as buy-and-hold, fix-and-flip, or rental properties, can further diversify your portfolio.

Setting Investment Milestones

Setting investment milestones is important for tracking your progress and staying motivated. *Define specific goals and milestones that you aim to achieve at different stages of your investment journey.* These milestones can include acquiring a certain number of properties, achieving a target cash flow, or reaching a certain net worth. By setting milestones, you can create a roadmap and measure your success over time. Regularly review and adjust these milestones as you progress and as market conditions evolve.

Leveraging Financing Options

Leveraging financing options can help accelerate your real estate investment plan. Real estate offers various financing avenues, including mortgages, loans, partnerships, and creative financing options. *Explore different financing options and evaluate their suitability based on your financial situation and investment goals.* Leverage can amplify your returns and allow you to acquire properties that may be beyond your immediate financial capacity. However, ensure that you carefully assess the risks and obligations associated with each financing option before proceeding.

Managing Cash Flow

Managing cash flow is essential for maintaining the financial health of your real estate investments. Evaluate the cash flow potential of each property in your portfolio, taking into account rental income, operating expenses, and debt service payments. Ensure that your rental income covers all expenses and allows for positive cash flow. Implement effective property management practices, such as tenant screening, rent collection, and regular property maintenance, to optimize cash flow and minimize vacancies. *Regularly monitor your cash flow and make necessary adjustments* to maintain a sustainable and profitable investment plan.

In conclusion, creating a long-term investment plan in real estate financing requires building a diversified portfolio, setting investment milestones, leveraging financing options, and managing cash flow effectively. By diversifying your investments, setting clear goals, exploring financing opportunities, and maintaining positive cash flow, you can increase the likelihood of long-term success in real estate investments. Regularly review and adjust your plan as market conditions evolve, and consult professionals for advice and guidance when needed. With a solid long-term investment plan in place, you can work towards achieving your financial goals and building wealth over time.

Conclusion: Last Part

In conclusion, real estate financing is a crucial aspect of successful real estate investing. By understanding loan options, setting clear investment goals, assessing risk tolerance, identifying opportunities, and creating a long-term investment plan, investors can navigate the financing landscape with confidence and increase their chances of success. Diligence, knowledge, and careful planning are essential, along with staying updated on market trends and seeking professional advice when needed. With these strategies in place, investors can unlock the full potential of their real estate investments and achieve their financial goals.

About The Author

JIM PELLERIN started real estate investing over twenty years ago. Since then, he has bought and sold millions of dollars of real estate. He began by purchasing and renting out duplexes. Following that he added Lease Options to his strategy. He has implemented many creative funding strategies that have allowed him to continue implementing various strategies and alloqed him to build a sizable portfolio.

As part of his education, he has attended numerous seminars on real estate investing, project management, property management, financing, renovations, motivation, time management, and many more. He has also read over 500 books on similar topics.

This book blends his experience and the knowledge he has gained through his investments and studies.

Visit his author page to discover my other publications: books2read.com/JimPellerin[1]

1. https://books2read.com/JimPellerin

Other Books By Jim Pellerin

Real Estate Investing: Strategies – The Secret to Financial Independence with Real Estate

books2read.com/strategies[1]

1. https://books2read.com/strategies

Real Estate Investing with Lease Options – How to Invest with No Money Down

books2read.com/Lease-Options[2]

2. https://books2read.com/Lease-Options

Invest NOW – The Passive Approach to Winning with Real Estate

books2read.com/investnow[3]

3. https://books2read.com/investnow

books2read.com/JimPellerin[4]

4. https://books2read.com/JimPellerin

Don't miss out!

Visit the website below and you can sign up to receive emails whenever Jim Pellerin publishes a new book. There's no charge and no obligation.

https://books2read.com/r/B-A-WGIX-RYHJC

BOOKS 2 READ

Connecting independent readers to independent writers.

Did you love *Ultimate Beginners Guide to Real Estate Investing Financing*? Then you should read *Real Estate Investing Strategies: The Secret to Financial Independence with Real Estate*[5] by Jim Pellerin!

[6]

The mechanics of Real Estate Investing is simple: Buy a house and do something with it. Fix it and rent it, or just sell it. Sounds simple, doesn't it? Yet only a small percentage of us have enough courage to go out and take advantage of the opportunities that are available to us. Real Estate Investing can be more promising than stocks, bonds, and various other securities because of the higher rates of return.

In this book, I show you how to get started by describing the different types of skills you need, by showing you how to take control of your personal and financial situation, and by helping you decide what type of real estate investing you want to get involved in. I also show

5. https://books2read.com/u/m2QyNG

6. https://books2read.com/u/m2QyNG

you how to find properties, how to analyze them, and how to make an offer that makes sense. And finally, I describe what you need to do to manage your investment and ultimately how to sell your investment for the most profit.

I have been involved in real estate investing for over 20 years. I have yet to find a book that focuses on the investor and the overall process. Sure, there are lots of books on fix and flips, buy, rent and hold, rent to own, etc. However, I haven't found any good books on how to really get started in the real estate investing process from a practical viewpoint. The technical aspects of real estate investing are really quite easy. But if it's so easy, then why isn't everyone doing it?

This book is for people who are serious about getting started in real estate investing and who want to join the 5% of those who actually take action and invest. This book provides a strategic approach with the tried and tested methods and principles that have helped others make millions in real estate.

Read more at www.jimpellerin.com.

Also by Jim Pellerin

Real Estate Investing

Real Estate Investing Strategies: The Secret to Financial Independence with Real Estate

Real Estate Investing with Lease Options - Investing in Real Estate with No Money Down

Invest Now - The Passive Approach to Winning at Real Estate

The Ultimate Beginners Guide to Real Estate Investing

The 98 Best Real Estate Investing Strategies

The Ultimate Beginners Guide to Wholesale Real Estate Investing

The Ultimate Beginners Guide to Rental Real Estate Investing

The Ultimate Beginners Guide to Fix and Flip Real Estate Investing

The Ultimate Beginners Guide to Private Equity Real Estate Investing

Ultimate Beginners Guide to Real Estate Investing Financing

Watch for more at www.jimpellerin.com.

www.ingramcontent.com/pod-product-compliance
Lightning Source LLC
LaVergne TN
LVHW052307200926
848481LV00002B/493
* 9 7 9 8 2 2 3 7 9 0 0 2 0 *